Book 2

40 DAYS

Prayers *and* Devotions to Revive *Your* Experience *With* God

D E N N I S   S M I T H

REVIEW AND HERALD® PUBLISHING ASSOCIATION

Since 1861 | www.reviewandherald.com

Also by Dennis Smith:
40 Days: Prayers and Devotions to Prepare for the Second Coming (KJV Edition)
40 Days: Prayers and Devotions to Prepare for the Second Coming (NKJV Edition)

To order, call **1-800-765-6955**.

Visit us at **www.reviewandherald.com**
for information on other Review and Herald® products.

Copyright © 2011 by Review and Herald® Publishing Association
Published by Review and Herald® Publishing Association, Hagerstown, MD 21741-1119

This book was
Edited by Kalie Kelch
Copyedited by James Hoffer
Designed by Ron J. Pride
Typeset: Times New Roman 11.6/15.6

PRINTED IN U.S.A.

15 14 13 12 11   5 4 3 2

Library of Congress Cataloging-in-Publication Data
Smith, Dennis Edwin, 1944-
  40 days. Book 2 : prayers and devotions to revive your experience with God / Dennis Smith.
    p. cm.
1. Spiritual life–Seventh-Day Adventists. 2. Seventh-Day Adventists–Prayers and devotions. I. Title. II. Title: Forty days. III. Title: Prayers and devotions to revive your experience with God.
  BV4501.3.S646 2010
  242'.2–dc22
                    2010017798

ISBN 978-0-8280-2550-8

Contents

A Note From the Author

This second 40 days book (Book 1, *40 Days: Prayers and Devotions to Prepare for the Second Coming,* published 2009) focuses on the relationship with God that His people must have in order to be ready for Christ's second coming. The reasons for the trials and difficult times God's children go through are explained. The importance of understanding God's sovereignty is presented, along with other vital biblical teachings for God's last generation to understand.

We have just begun a second 40 days in our New Haven, Connecticut, church, and already I can see how important it is to have a second devotional for the participants to use. This second 40 days devotional will be an important resource for a second 40 days spiritual emphasis in your church. You will find that it builds on the lessons in the first 40 days devotional.

Introduction

This 40-days-of-study-and-prayer devotional is the second one in the series of 40-day devotionals. As with the first one, *40 Days: Prayers and Devotions to Prepare for the Second Coming,* this devotional is designed to prepare God's church for Christ's second coming as well as reach out to others in preparation for that glorious event. This preparation begins with church members who are willing to commit to 40 days of prayer and devotional study to develop a closer personal relationship with Jesus Christ, and to reach out to five individuals whom the Lord has put on their heart to pray for every day.

Jesus said, "If two of you agree on earth concerning anything that they ask, it will be done for them by My Father in heaven" (Matt. 18:19). There is great power in united prayer, and there is encouragement and spiritual strength found in Christian fellowship.

First, all who prayerfully enter into the 40 days of personal devotional study and prayer will strengthen their relationship with the Lord. They will grow in the Spirit–filled experience, and their prayer life will become more consistent and effective.

Second, prayer for those on the prayer list will enable the Holy Spirit to work in the lives of those prayed for in bringing them closer to Christ. Members will be encouraged as they see the Spirit answering their prayers.

In order to get the greatest benefit from this devotional book, it is suggested that you find a prayer partner to fellowship with and pray together with, either on the phone or in person, every day during the 40 days of prayer and study. In addition, it is recommended that you find several individuals who are also involved in the program to form a small group that can meet together in weekly study and prayer.

The devotional studies are divided into five sections. Each section describes experiences God's people have when they are ready for Christ's second coming. Each devotional study is followed by personal reflection and discussion questions.

If you want to develop a closer relationship with Jesus and reach out to those whom God has put on your heart who have either once known the truth of God's Word and have slipped away, or have never known the warning message God is giving to prepare the world for Christ's soon return, this book is for you.

Getting Started

As you prepare to embark on this journey, there are a few steps to follow:

1. Find a prayer partner. You will be contacting your prayer partner each day to do the following:

1. Share insights on the reading for the day.
2. Discuss the personal reflection and discussion questions.
3. Pray for each other.
4. Encourage each other to pray for the five people you each have on your list.
5. Remind each other to show the five people on your list that you care.

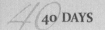

2. **Pray that God will show you whom you should be praying for.** During the 40 days you will be praying for five people. Ask God for guidance as you select these individuals.

3. **Choose five people to pray for.** Those on your prayer list may be family members, friends, or coworkers. They may be individuals who have either left the church, or were never members of the church. (They should be individuals living in your area in order to invite them to church sometime during the next 40 days.)

4. **Contact each of the five people you have selected.** You may choose to contact these individuals in person, by phone, by e-mail, or by mail. Following is sample text you can use when contacting the individuals you have selected:

Beginning _____ my church is having a special emphasis on prayer, and is requesting that we choose five individuals to pray for during the next 40 days.

Since you are _____ (examples: my friend, my neighbor, my coworker) it seemed only natural that I would think of praying for you. I would be honored if you would let me know what your specific prayer requests are so that I can know how to pray for you for the next 40 days.

I hope to hear from you soon. I'll keep in touch. Thank you, and God bless!

5. **Create a prayer card for each individual to keep you on track.** Following is a sample card:

Name: _____

Phone: _____

E-mail: _____

_____

Address: _____

_____

Prayer Requests: _____

_____

_____

_____

40 Days of Prayer: _____

_____

_____

_____

_____

Caring Activities: _____

_____

_____

_____

6. Pray for these individuals every day. As you pray, claim the scriptures below on their behalf. These are taken from *The Praying Church Sourcebook*, pages 128, 129.

1. That God will draw them to Himself (John 6:44).

2. That they seek to know God (Acts 17:27).

3. That they believe the Word of God (1 Thess. 2:13).

4. That Satan be bound from blinding them to the truth and that his influences in their life be "cast down" (2 Cor. 4:4; 10:4, 5).

5. That the Holy Spirit work in them (John 16:8-13).

6. That they turn from sin (Acts 3:19).

7. That they believe in Christ as Savior (John 1:12).

8. That they obey Christ as Lord (Matt. 7:21).

9. That they take root and grow in Christ (Col. 2:6, 7).

7. Prayerfully consider what activities you can do to show you care. The following list contains suggestions of things you can do for those on your prayer list to show that you care for them. Add to this list as the Lord leads.

1. Tell them what you appreciate about them.

2. Send them a piece of encouraging literature.

3. Call and pray with them.

4. Invite them to dinner at your home.

5. Invite them to go out to lunch with you.

6. Send them a birthday card.

7. Send them a card expressing encouragement or what God puts in your heart.

8. Take them something you cooked.

9. Invite them to go shopping or to a museum, etc.

10. Send them a get well or sympathy card when needed.

11. Give their child a birthday card and gift when appropriate.

12. Invite them to attend church with you.

13. At the appropriate time ask if they would like to receive Bible studies.

The Power of Prayer

Prayer is the most powerful force on earth. It is essential for one's personal spiritual growth and is the most effective means of reaching others for Christ. Concerning prayer and the Christian's spiritual growth, Ellen White wrote:

"Prayer is the breath of the soul. It is the secret of spiritual power. No other means of grace can be substituted, and the health of the soul be preserved. Prayer brings the heart into immediate contact with the Well-spring of life, and strengthens the sinew and muscle of the religious experience" (*Gospel Workers*, p. 254, 255).

Mrs. White also recognized the necessity of prayer in leading others to Christ:

"Through much prayer you must labor for souls, for this is the only method by which you can reach hearts. It is not your work, but the work of Christ who is by your side, that impresses hearts" (*Evangelism*, p. 342).

As you prayerfully work to bring others closer to Christ and His church, God will bless your efforts. When you pray for, and work for, those on your prayer list, God will not only use you to win others to Christ; He will draw you closer to Himself.

Ellen White understood this double blessing when she wrote:

"As you work to answer your own prayers, you will find that God will reveal Himself unto you. . . . Begin now to reach higher and still higher. Prize the things of heaven above earthly attractions and inducements. . . . Learn how to pray; learn how to bear a clear and intelligent testimony, and God will be glorified in you" (*The Upward Look*, p. 256).

"Their persevering prayers will bring souls to the cross. In cooperation with their self-sacrificing efforts Jesus will move upon hearts, working miracles in the conversion of souls" (*Testimonies for the Church*, vol. 7, p. 27).

To facilitate the prayer emphasis of this program, there is a "Prayer Activity" section at the end of each day's devotional that offers a suggested prayer focus for the day.

The Power of the Holy Spirit

After His resurrection, Jesus told His disciples that they were to wait to receive the baptism of the Holy Spirit before they went forth to proclaim the gospel to the world (Acts 1:4-8). Even though they had spent the past three and a half years daily with Christ and had seen and participated in a ministry of miracles, they were not ready to witness for Him. They were to wait to receive the power of the Holy Spirit. After they received the baptism of the Holy Spirit, which took place on the day of Pentecost, they were empowered as never before to witness for Christ:

"Now when the Day of Pentecost had fully come, they were all with one accord in one place. And suddenly there came a sound from heaven, as of a rushing mighty wind, and it filled the whole house where they were sitting. Then there appeared to them divided tongues, as of fire, and one sat upon each of them. And they were all filled with the Holy Spirit and began to speak with other tongues, as the Spirit gave them utterance" (Acts 2:1-4).

Because the baptism of the Holy Spirit (also called the infilling of the Spirit) is so vital to our personal spiritual growth and our witness to others, these 40 devotional lessons will be based on this important teaching in God's Word.

Your 40–Day Journey

The 40 devotional studies focus on practical biblical teachings that are important for every Christian to understand in order to faithfully serve Christ. Such subjects as the importance of experiencing the daily baptism of the Holy Spirit and righteousness by faith in Christ are presented. Also, you will study what it means to "wait" with trusting faith on God even through the most difficult situations. You will learn why it is important for Christians to understand the truths about God's sovereignty. If this is not understood, it will be much easier to get discouraged when trials and difficulties assail one's life. These and many other essential truths are presented in this book to strengthen God's people and prepare them for the final crisis and Christ's second coming.

By choosing to participate in the 40 days of study and prayer, you are entering into an amazing and blessed adventure with the Lord. You will experience a deeper relationship with Christ, and you will see the Lord use you to draw others closer to Himself in preparation for His soon return. As you fellowship with your prayer partner and the others participating in the program, you will experience a deeper Christian love and unity with your fellow believers. This will also play an important role in your personal spiritual growth.

In order to get the most from this experience, it is recommended that this be the first thing you do in the morning. It may require rising a little earlier, but the effort will be well rewarded. If you ask the Lord to wake you so you can have some quality time with Him, He will hear and answer your prayer. Concerning Christ's devotional life Ellen White wrote:

"Daily He received a fresh baptism of the Holy Spirit. In the early hours of the new day the Lord awakened Him from His slumbers, and His soul and His lips were anointed with grace, that He might impart to others. His words were given Him fresh from the heavenly courts, words that He might speak in season to the weary and oppressed" (*Christ's Object Lessons*, p. 139).

Christ will do the same for you if you ask Him. He very much desires to anoint you with His Spirit in preparation for each new day. This book is designed to facilitate just that—a daily anointing of God's Spirit for personal spiritual growth, and witnessing for Christ.

Other Benefits and Uses

The Lord can and will use this 40–day devotional study to benefit His work. It is recommended that this devotional be used in conjunction with an evangelistic effort. Fifty days before the meetings begin, church members should be invited to participate in the 40 days of devotional study and prayer. As part of their daily prayer focus, they should include the Visitor's Sabbath and/or evangelistic meetings. The Visitor's Sabbath is to be held at the end of the 40 days, with the evangelistic meetings starting shortly thereafter. The visitors are given a handbill of the evangelistic meetings on Visitor's Sabbath inviting them to attend the opening night.

Imagine the power of a large number of church members systematically praying for Visitor's Sabbath and the evangelistic meetings every day for 40 days. Plus, the five individuals placed on the individual prayer lists are to be invited to attend Visitor's Sabbath and the opening night of the evangelistic meetings. Church members will see many friends, family members, and former Adventists attend in response to their personal invitation supported by the daily prayers for these individuals.

This 40 days of devotional study and prayer focus will prove to be a blessing to any spiritual emphasis in the local church, whether a spiritual growth focus for the members or outreach efforts in the community.

A conference can also use the 40–day emphasis prior to a major conference-wide spiritual emphasis or evangelistic effort. Pastors and conference church members can join together in united study and prayer for the event.

Another effective use of the *40 Days* book is to go through it with new church members. The teachings in it are important for every Christian to understand and apply to their life. Therefore, the *40 Days* devotional can also be used following evangelistic meetings for the new converts. This would expose them to important biblical teachings to strengthen their walk with God, strengthen their connection to the church, and give the pastor or other lay leaders an opportunity to stay connected with them following the meetings. The new members could meet as a small group, weekly or more often, to review the studies. Also, a church member who has previously gone through the *40 Days* devotional could be assigned to be their prayer partner. This would be a good way to spiritually strengthen new members and connect them with the church and at least one other church member.

Note: 40 Days *is designed also to work along with "Light America Mission," a program of personal spiritual growth through the study of God's Word, prayer, training, and community outreach to share the three angels' messages.*

Information on how to conduct a 40 days program of devotional study and prayer in your church is available at www.40daysdevotional.com. A free downloadable instruction manual is located on the Web site.

" *Prayer* is the breath
of the soul. It is the secret
of spiritual power.
No other means of grace
can be substituted,
and the health of the soul
be preserved.
Prayer brings the heart
into immediate contact
with the Well-spring
of life..." (Gospel Workers, pp. 254, 255).

Day 1

The Amazing Born Again Experience

There are similarities and differences in the experience of every Christian. However, I believe there are three experiences in Christ that have the most profound influence and are the same for every Christian. Also, all three experiences are necessary in order to be ready for Christ's return. These three are the born again experience, Spirit baptism, and experiencing righteousness by faith in Christ. Revival will also be presented in this section of the devotional, which is necessary for God's people to come out of their Laodicean condition.

The first amazing experience every Christian has is the new birth under the power of the Holy Spirit. John referred to this born again experience in his Gospel:

"But as many as received Him, to them He gave the right to become children of God, to those who believe in His name: who were born, not of blood, nor of the will of the flesh, nor of the will of man, but of God" (John 1:12, 13).

"Jesus answered and said to him, 'Most assuredly, I say to you, unless one is born again, he cannot see the kingdom of God. . . . That which is born of the flesh is flesh, and that which is born of the Spirit is spirit' " (John 3:3, 6).

The born again experience comes at different times in a Christian's life. My encounter with Christ came when I was a senior engineering student in college. Its influence was so profound in my life that it totally changed my philosophy of life from worldly values to spiritual values. In time this experience led me to leave the profession of engineering to study for the ministry.

Every Christian has a similar experience that causes them to change their values and philosophy of life—a life changed from seeking worldly success to desiring to serve Christ and follow Him wherever He leads. The experience the apostle John describes takes place in the heart by faith:

"Do not love the world or the things in the world. If anyone loves the world, the love of the Father is not in him. For all that is in the world—the lust of the flesh, the lust of the eyes, and the pride of life—is not of the Father but is of the world. And the world is passing away, and the lust of it; but he who does the will of God abides forever" (1 John 2:15-17).

> ## Christians no longer love the world nor the things of the world.

The Christians no longer love the world nor the things of the world. They have received a new heart from God:

"Then I will sprinkle clean water on you, and you shall be clean; I will cleanse you from all your filthiness and from all your idols. I will give you a new heart and put a new spirit within you; I will take the heart of stone out of your flesh and give you a heart of flesh. I will put My Spirit within you and cause you to walk in My statutes, and you will keep My judgments and do them" (Eze. 36:25-27).

When one accepts Christ, he is forgiven and cleansed from all his sins:

"If we confess our sins, He is faithful and just to

forgive us our sins, and to cleanse us from all unrighteousness" (1 John 1:9).

The new believer is not only forgiven of all sin, but receives the promise of eternal life:

"And this is the testimony: that God has given us eternal life, and this life is in His Son. He who has the Son has life; he who does not have the Son of God does not have life. These things I have written to you who believe in the name of the Son of God, that you may know that you have eternal life, and that you may continue to believe in the name of the Son of God" (1 John 5:11-13).

If you have not accepted Christ as your Savior, I invite you to do so right now. You can pray the following simple prayer:

"Father, I accept Jesus Christ as my personal Savior. I ask You to forgive me for all my sins and cleanse me from all unrighteousness. I accept Your promise of eternal life. Thank you for forgiving me and giving me eternal life through Jesus. In Jesus' name, amen."

Or if you have wandered away from Christ, I invite you to renew your relationship with Him. I invite you to pray the following prayer:

"Father, I accept Jesus Christ anew as my Savior. I ask You to forgive me for all my sins and cleanse me from all unrighteousness. I accept Your promise to give me eternal life. Thank you for forgiving me and for the assurance I have of spending eternity with you. In Jesus' name, amen."

Personal Reflection and Discussion

1. How does a person become born again?

_____

_____

2. When did you experience being born again? How did you feel after the experience?

_____

_____

3. What happens in one's life when he/she experiences the new birth by the Spirit?

_____

_____

4. How has the born again experience changed your life?

_____

_____

Prayer Activity

- **Call your prayer partner and discuss this devotional with him/her.**
- **Pray with your prayer partner:**
    1. **for God to renew your born again relationship with Him every day.**
    2. **for God to open your understanding as you study your daily devotional.**
    3. **for God to bless you and your prayer partner's fellowship.**
    4. **for the individuals on your prayer list.**

Day 2

The Amazing Spirit Baptized Experience

The second amazing experience God wants every Christian to have is the baptism of the Holy Spirit. Being born again is one thing; being baptized by the Holy Spirit is another.

The disciples were converted to Jesus, but they were powerless before the day of Pentecost. So Jesus commanded them to wait in prayer until they received the baptism of the Holy Spirit. Wait for the Promise of the Father, 'which,' He said, 'you have heard from Me; for John truly baptized with water, but you shall be baptized with the Holy Spirit not many days from now. . . . But you shall receive power when the Holy Spirit has come upon you; and you shall be witnesses to Me in Jerusalem, and in all Judea and Samaria, and to the end of the earth' " (Acts 1:4-8).

"Now when the Day of Pentecost was fully come, they were all with one accord in one place. And suddenly there came a sound from heaven, as of a rushing mighty wind, and it filled the whole house where they were sitting. Then there appeared to them divided tongues, as of fire, and one sat upon each of them. And they were all filled with the Holy Spirit and began to speak with other tongues, as the Spirit gave them utterance" (Acts 2:1-4).

The experience of being baptized by the Spirit gave great power to the disciples' teaching and preaching. Three thousand accepted Jesus and were baptized in water following Peter's sermon on the day of Pentecost.

When a Christian receives the baptism of the Holy Spirit, he/she will be empowered to serve God more effectively and reveal Christ more fully in his/her life. Of this Ellen White wrote:

"Impress upon all the necessity of the baptism of the Holy Spirit, the sanctification of the church, so that they will be living, growing, fruit-bearing trees of the Lord's planting" (*Testimonies for the Church,* vol. 6, p. 86).

In order for Christians to grow spiritually, they must daily experience the baptism of the Holy Spirit. Ellen White wrote of Jesus' recognition of this vital truth:

"Daily He received a fresh baptism of the Holy Spirit. In the early hours of the new day the Lord awakened Him from His slumbers, and His soul and His lips were anointed with grace, that He might impart to others" (*Christ's Object Lessons*, p. 139).

The apostle Paul actually commands the Christian to "keep on" being filled with the Spirit, which must be a daily experience:

"And do not be drunk with wine, in which is dissipation; but be filled with the Spirit" (Eph. 5:18).

The Greek verb form for "be filled" is "keep on being filled," a continuous action verb. Spirit baptism is not a one-time experience. It is to be a daily experience in the Christian's life.

If you have never asked God to baptize you with His Spirit, I invite you to do so now by praying the following prayer: "Father, I thank You for leading me to accept Jesus Christ as my Savior, and I ask You to forgive me for all my sins. I desire to commit my life 100 percent to Jesus. I claim the promise of the baptism of the Holy Spirit in my life right now. Father, fill me with Your Spirit and manifest in me every fruit of the Spirit. I pray that You will so infill me with the presence of Jesus that His character will be fully manifested through me. I claim Your promise to empower me by Your Spirit to serve You as You lead me into ministry for Jesus. In Jesus' name, amen."

Personal Reflection and Discussion

1. What did Jesus ask the disciples to wait for before they went forth to witness for Him?

_____

_____

2. What did the baptism of the Holy Spirit do in the lives of the disciples?

_____

_____

3. Why did Ellen White say we need the baptism of the Holy Spirit?

_____

_____

4. How often did Jesus seek the baptism of the Holy Spirit and why?

_____

_____

5. How often should the Christian seek the baptism of the Holy Spirit? Why is this important?

_____

_____

Prayer Activity

- Call your prayer partner and discuss this devotional with him/her.
- Pray with your prayer partner:
    1. for God to baptize you with His Holy Spirit.
    2. for God to manifest the fruits of the Spirit in your life.
    3. for God to manifest the gifts of the Spirit in your life that He has chosen for you.
    4. for the individuals on your prayer list.

Day 3

The Amazing Christ Our Righteousness Experience

The third most amazing experience in a Christian's life is the discovery of the justification and sanctification aspect of righteousness by faith. This experience is not often discovered immediately, but after seeking God and struggling ineffectively with one's besetting sins, we will grasp the concept.

Justification means that God frees the believer from the guilt and penalty of sin and covers the repentant sinner with the righteousness (perfect obedience) of Christ.

"If we confess our sins, He is faithful and just to forgive us our sins and to cleanse us from all unrighteousness" (1 John 1:9).

God's forgiveness is so complete that He says:

"Their sins and their lawless deeds I will remember no more" (Heb. 10:17).

"As far as the east is from the west, so far has He removed our transgressions from us" (Ps. 103:12).

Sanctification refers to the biblical truth that Jesus not only imputes His righteousness to you through justification, but He also imparts His righteousness to you for everyday living. Christ is not only a sin-pardoning Savior but a sin-delivering Savior. This happens as Christians learn to let Jesus live out His obedient life in and through them.

It is through the baptism of the Holy Spirit that Christ lives in the believer:

"And I will pray the Father, and He will give you another Helper, that He may abide with you forever, even the Spirit of truth, whom the world cannot receive, because it neither sees Him nor knows Him; but you know Him, for He dwells with you and will be in you. I will not leave you orphans; **I will come to you**" (John 14:16-18, emphasis added).

Jesus wants to live out His life of obedience in every Christian. When we are tempted He wants us to turn to Him and ask Him to manifest His obedience in that area of our life. That is how the Christian experiences Christ's sanctifying righteousness.

"For what the law could not do in that it was weak through the flesh, God did by sending His own Son in the likeness of sinful flesh, on account of sin: He condemned sin in the flesh, that the righteous requirement of the law might be fulfilled in us who do not walk according to the flesh but according to the Spirit" (Rom. 8:3, 4).

Notice that this scripture states that the "righteous requirement of the law" is to be fulfilled "in" us, not "by" us. As we learn how to let Jesus live out His righteous life in and through our daily life, we will experience immense joy. Christ's justifying righteousness and sanctifying righteousness is our only hope of being righteous, our only hope of glorifying God.

"To them God willed to make known what are the riches of the glory of this mystery among the Gentiles: which is Christ in you, the hope of glory" (Col. 1:27).

When tempted the Christian is to look to Jesus alone for deliverance:

"Let us lay aside every weight, and the sin which so easily ensnares us, and let us run with endurance the race that is set before us, looking unto Jesus, the author and finisher of our faith" (Heb. 12:1, 2).

The three experiences described in the first three days of this devotional study are more amazing and life–changing than anything else in this world. They are necessary experiences for those ready to meet Jesus when He returns. May you experience all three to the fullest in your life.

Personal Reflection and Discussion

1. What does Christ's justifying righteousness do for the believer?

_____

_____

2. When does the Christian usually experience the third amazing experience of Christ's sanctifying righteousness?

_____

_____

3. How does Jesus live in Christians? How does He live in you?

_____

_____

4. What is the Christian to do in relation to Christ to overcome temptation?

_____

_____

5. What are the three amazing experiences described in the first three devotionals?

_____

_____

Prayer Activity

- Call your prayer partner and discuss this devotional with him/her.
- Pray with your prayer partner:
    1. for God to baptize you with His Holy Spirit.
    2. for Jesus to live out His righteous life in you every day.
    3. for God to remind you to look to Jesus when you are tempted.
    4. for the individuals on your prayer list.

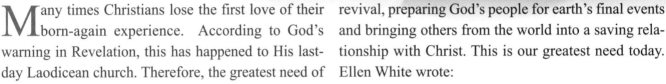

Day 4

The Amazing Experience of Revival: Part 1

Many times Christians lose the first love of their born-again experience. According to God's warning in Revelation, this has happened to His last-day Laodicean church. Therefore, the greatest need of God's people today is revival:

"So then, because you are lukewarm, and neither cold nor hot, I will spew you out of My mouth. Because you say, 'I am rich, have become wealthy, and have need of nothing'—and do not know that you are wretched, miserable, poor, blind, and naked" (Rev. 3:16, 17).

Likewise, the greatest need of the world today is revival. The world has reached the point of such degraded immorality that it is ripe for God's judgments. History reveals that every nation that followed this path ended in destruction. Daniel's prophecy in chapter 2 of his book reveals that all the nations at the end of time will be arrayed against God. That is why God pictured a "stone" striking the prophetic image on its feet:

"And in the days of these kings the God of heaven will set up a kingdom which shall never be destroyed; and the kingdom shall not be left to other people; it shall break in pieces and consume all these kingdoms, and it shall stand forever. Inasmuch as you saw that the stone was cut out of the mountain without hands, and that it broke in pieces the iron, the bronze, the clay, the silver, and the gold" (Dan. 2:44, 45).

The events taking place in our world today call for God to intervene:

"It is time for You to act, O Lord, for they have regarded Your law as void" (Ps. 119:126).

Don't ever doubt it; God will act to bring an end to sin in this world, which will happen when Christ returns. However, before that time there must be a great revival, preparing God's people for earth's final events and bringing others from the world into a saving relationship with Christ. This is our greatest need today. Ellen White wrote:

"A revival of true godliness among us is the greatest and most urgent of all our needs. To seek this should be our first work" (*Selected Messages*, book 1, p. 121).

On the day of Pentecost, a great revival broke out in the church. Joy filled each heart and the good news about Christ spread rapidly, bringing salvation to multitudes of people.

"When the Day of Pentecost had fully come, they were all with one accord in one place. And suddenly there came a sound from heaven, as of a rushing mighty wind, and it filled the whole house where they were sitting. Then there appeared to them divided tongues, as of fire, and one sat upon each of them. And they were all filled with the Holy Spirit and began to speak with other tongues, as the Spirit gave them utterance. Now there were dwelling in Jerusalem Jews, devout men, from every nation under heaven. And when this sound occurred, the multitude came together, and were confused, because everyone heard them speak in his own language. Then they were all amazed and marveled, saying to one another, 'Look, are not all these who speak Galileans? . . . We hear them speaking in our own tongues the wonderful works of God.'

"Then those who gladly received his word were baptized; and that day about three thousand souls were added to them. . . . So continuing daily with one accord in the temple, and breaking bread from house to house, they ate their food with gladness and simplicity of heart, praising God and having favor with all the people. And the Lord added to the church daily those who were being saved" (Acts 2:1-11, 41-47).

Here we see that when revival took place the church was filled with joy. They loved one another and longed to fellowship together every day. They had one purpose in life: to share Jesus with others. As a result thousands joined the church; every day the "Lord added to the church."

We, like David, need to cry out to God to bring about a great revival in our midst today:

"Will You not revive us again, that Your people may rejoice in You?" (Ps. 85:6).

Personal Reflection and Discussion

1. What is the greatest need of the church today? Do you have this same need?

_____

_____

2. Why does the church need to experience revival?

_____

_____

3. What changes occur in the church when revival takes place?

_____

_____

4. What impact does the church have on the community when revival takes place?

_____

_____

Prayer Activity

- **Call your prayer partner and discuss this devotional with him/her.**
- **Pray with your prayer partner:**
    1. **for God to baptize you with His Holy Spirit.**
    2. **for God to revive you and His church.**
    3. **for God to lead many to accept Jesus.**
    4. **for those on your prayer list.**

Day 5

The Amazing Experience of Revival: Part 2

Revival does not occur because of something we do as Christians. Revival is the result of God working in our midst. However, there are things Christians must do in order for revival to take place. There is an inseparable relationship between revival and the baptism of the Holy Spirit. Ellen White wrote:

"The baptism of the Holy Ghost as on the day of Pentecost will lead to a revival of true religion and the performance of many wonderful works" (*Selected Messages*, book 2, p. 57).

The baptism of the Holy Spirit spiritually revives the Laodicean Christian and gives him/her the power to witness for Christ. Jesus certainly knew the importance of what would happen when the Holy Spirit would be poured out in the "early rain" power on the day of Pentecost. Speaking of this He said:

"I have come to bring fire on the earth, and how I wish it were already kindled!" (Luke 12:49, NIV).

What fire was Jesus speaking of? Of course, He was speaking about the fire of the Holy Spirit.

"John answered, saying to all, 'I indeed baptize you with water; but One mightier than I is coming, whose sandal strap I am not worthy to loose. He will baptize you with the Holy Spirit and fire' " (Luke 3:16).

How do Laodicean Christians receive the baptism of the Holy Spirit and experience revival? The same way believers always have—by prayerfully claiming God's promise. The baptism of the Holy Spirit was received by the early church on the day of Pentecost as a result of them praying together for 10 days, claiming Christ's promise:

"These all continued with one accord in prayer and supplication, with the women and Mary the mother of Jesus, and with His brothers" (Acts 1:14).

Ellen White confirmed the necessity of prayer for revival to take place when she wrote: "A revival need be expected only in answer to prayer" (*Selected Messages*, book 1, p. 121).

Every Christian today needs to pray the prayer of David that I mentioned at the close of yesterday's devotional: "Will You not revive us again, That Your people may rejoice in You?" (Ps. 85:6).

Revival was not reserved for the early Christian church. In the book of 2 Chronicles we read a very clear description of how revival takes place among God's people.

"If My people who are called by My name will humble themselves, and pray and seek My face, and turn from their wicked ways, then I will hear from heaven, and will forgive their sin and heal their land" (2 Chron. 7:14).

God is ready and willing to pour out His Spirit, but revival requires 100 percent surrender to God on our part. That is why in God's message to the Laodiceans He counsels them to "buy" of Him:

"I counsel you to buy from Me gold refined in the fire, that you may be rich; and white garments, that you may be clothed, that the shame of your nakedness may not be revealed; and anoint your eyes with eye salve, that you may see" (Rev. 3:18).

We "buy" by giving ourselves unreservedly to God. There may be financial wrongs to be righted, which may cost us money. There may be apologies to be given, which will cost us our pride. However, if you want to make the devil tremble, begin earnestly to seek God for revival:

"There is nothing that Satan fears so much as that the people of God shall clear the way by removing every hindrance, so that the Lord can pour out His Spirit upon a languishing church and an impenitent congregation" (*Selected Messages*, book 1, p. 124).

Are you willing to surrender all to God and "buy" of Him by giving Him 100 percent of yourself? That is what it will take to experience revival in your life and be part of the great revival that will soon take place among God's people.

Personal Reflection and Discussion

1. **What attitude must Christians have toward God for revival to take place in their life?**

_____

_____

2. **What two things must Christians do in order for revival to take place? Have you done these two things?**

_____

_____

3. **What did David pray for?**

_____

_____

4. **What will the baptism of the Holy Spirit do for Christians and the church? Why is this important?**

_____

_____

Prayer Activity

- **Call your prayer partner and discuss this devotional with him/her.**
- **Pray with your prayer partner:**
    1. **for God to baptize you with His Holy Spirit.**
    2. **for God to give you the desire to surrender 100 percent to Him.**
    3. **for God to revive you and His church.**
    4. **for those on your prayer list.**

Day 6

The Amazing Experience of Revival: Part 3

Revival is a time when the Christian's life is renewed in Christ. The joy of salvation fills the heart and a burden for soul-winning burns within. The revived Christian longs to see others come to accept Christ. When revival comes, those experiencing revival want to meet together to sing praises to God, to pray, and to study God's Word. When the church is revived, a new life and vibrancy infuses it—it is the very life of Jesus.

When a church is revived, the effects spill into the community in which the revival is happening. Sinners begin feeling a deep conviction of sin. These convicted sinners begin coming to the church to learn more about Jesus. In addition the revived Christians will be daily reaching out to the unsaved with prayer and will be personally sharing Jesus with them.

Experiencing the baptism of the Holy Spirit on a daily basis and having an active prayer life are the only pathways to revival. However, this will happen only after Christians surrender 100 percent of their life to God—every area and aspect of their life is His.

The great revivalist, Ruben Torrey, of the late 1800s to early 1900s gave the following prescription for revival, which includes three basic requirements:

Let a few Christians get thoroughly right with God. If this is not done, the rest will come to nothing.

Let them bind themselves together to pray for revival until God opens the windows of heaven and comes down.

Let them put themselves at the disposal of God for His use as He sees fit in winning others to Christ.

We can clearly see from God's Word and Christian writers of the past that total surrender to God, prayer, the baptism of the Holy Spirit, revival, and evangelism all go hand in hand. If any one of these ingredients is missing in our Christian experience, then we are not where God wants us to be in our walk with Him. These and only these ingredients will bring today's Christian from the state of "lukewarm" Laodicea to a state of giving life to all with whom they come into contact. When this happens in believers' lives, they will begin to see God use them as never before to bring men and women into the kingdom of God.

It is by receiving the baptism of the Holy Spirit that Jesus fully dwells in us:

"And I will pray the Father, and He will give you another Helper, that He may abide with you forever, even the Spirit of truth, whom the world cannot receive, because it neither sees Him nor knows Him; but you know Him, for He dwells with you and will be in you. I will not leave you orphans; I will come to you" (John 14:16-18).

When Jesus lives in us via the baptism of the Holy Spirit, He will begin living out His life in us. He will begin ministering to others through us. Hence, as Jesus brought life to those He met and ministered to, so we will also bring life in ministry just as Jesus did.

Jesus described this when He stated: "He who believes in Me, as the Scripture has said, out of his heart will flow rivers of living water" (John 7:38). The inspired commentary on this states: "But this He spoke concerning the Spirit, whom those believing in Him would receive; for the Holy Spirit was not yet given, because Jesus was not yet glorified" (John 7:39). The Bible clearly indicates in these verses that a Spirit-filled believer will bring life to his world because he will have "rivers of living water" flowing from him.

This is why Jesus told the disciples to "wait" for the baptism of the Holy Spirit. He knows that without this Spirit infilling the church we would be powerless and not bring life to those we come into contact with. However, when the church is Spirit–filled, the believers will then experience revival and "receive power" to witness for their Lord: "But you shall receive power when the Holy Spirit has come upon you; and you shall be witnesses to Me in Jerusalem, and in all Judea and Samaria, and to the end of the earth" (Acts 1:8).

Personal Reflection and Discussion

1. Describe what takes place when a Christian and church experience revival.

_____

_____

2. What was Ruben Torrey's prescription for revival to take place?

_____

_____

3. Why did Jesus tell the disciples to wait before they began witnessing for Him?

_____

_____

4. What will Jesus do when He dwells in the Christian through the baptism of the Holy Spirit?

_____

_____

Prayer Activity

- Call your prayer partner and discuss this devotional with him/her.
- Pray with your prayer partner:
    1. for God to baptize you with His Holy Spirit.
    2. for God to give you the desire to experience revival.
    3. for God to revive you and His church.
    4. for those on your prayer list.

Day 7

The Amazing Experience of Revival: Part 4

We see powerful, Spirit-filled witnessing taking place in the early church. We read of thousands accepting Christ and becoming part of God's church:

"Then those who gladly received his word were baptized; and that day about three thousand souls were added to them. . . . However, many of those who heard the word believed; and the number of the men came to be about five thousand" (Acts 2:41; 4:4).

We also read of just how life-giving the church was to those who joined the church:

"And through the hands of the apostles many signs and wonders were done among the people. And they were all with one accord in Solomon's Porch. . . . And believers were increasingly added to the Lord, multitudes of both men and women, so that they brought the sick out into the streets and laid them on beds and couches, that at least the shadow of Peter passing by might fall on some of them. Also a multitude gathered from the surrounding cities to Jerusalem, bringing sick people and those who were tormented by unclean spirits, and they were all healed" (Acts 5:12, 14-16).

Why was the church such a powerful influence in the world? It was a direct result of Jesus living in it through the baptism of the Holy Spirit. He was doing the works of ministry He did when on earth. The church truly became the "body of Christ" on earth as a result of receiving the Spirit's infilling on the day of Pentecost.

The problem with Laodicean, last-day Christians is that we don't realize our true condition. We think that everything is fine: "Because you say, 'I am rich, have become wealthy, and have need of nothing'—and do not know that you are wretched, miserable, poor, blind, and naked" (Rev. 3:17).

There is only one way for this self-deception to be broken. We must let Jesus come fully into our lives through the baptism of the Holy Spirit: "Behold, I stand at the door and knock. If anyone hears My voice and opens the door, I will come in to him and dine with him, and he with Me" (Rev. 3:20).

When we seek and receive the infilling of the Holy Spirit, our eyes will be opened and we will begin to see our true condition before God:

"I counsel you to buy from Me gold refined in the fire, that you may be rich; and white garments, that you may be clothed, that the shame of your nakedness may not be revealed; and anoint your eyes with eye salve, that you may see" (Rev. 3:18).

This verse gives the solution to the Laodicean church's problem—Jesus counsels us to buy His gold. We accomplish this task by giving ourselves 100 percent to God. The gold refers to the character of faith and love of righteousness of Jesus that is to become an integral part of the Christian's everyday life. This can happen only as the Christian is filled with the Holy Spirit and learns how to let Jesus live out His life in him/her. Christ wants to live out His righteous life of love and faith within the believer. Therefore, in this counsel to the Laodiceans, God is calling His church to experience the sanctification aspect of righteousness by faith; to experience Jesus as a sin-delivering Savior.

God also counsels the Laodicean Christians to buy the "white raiment," which refers to the covering righteousness of Christ that is experienced when the Christian enters into the justified experience Christ offers. Only righteous individuals will be saved. Christians can become righteous before God only by accepting

Jesus Christ as their Savior and being covered with His righteous obedience to God. Hence, through Christ the sinner is "clothed" with Christ's "white raiment" of perfect righteousness. The only righteousness in this earth is Christ's righteousness.

In God's counsel to the Laodiceans, we see that only through understanding and experiencing the baptism of the Holy Spirit and righteousness by faith (justifying and sanctifying righteousness) will we come out of our Laodicean condition and experience revival.

Revelation describes a time when the earth will be lighted with God's glory: "After these things I saw another angel coming down from heaven, having great authority, and the earth was illuminated with his glory" (Rev. 18:1). This will happen just before Jesus comes, and it describes a time when Christ's character will be perfectly reflected through His people to all the earth. Spirit-filled believers will be reflecting God's glory (character) to those around them. Just as Jesus' character drew men and women to Himself when He walked this earth, so Jesus will draw men and women to Himself by living in and ministering through Spirit-filled believers. This will be the glorious result of the church experiencing the last great revival. God is calling us to this revival experience today.

Personal Reflection and Discussion

1. How did the revived church described in the first few chapters of Acts impact their community?

_____

_____

2. What is the Laodicean Christian's problem today, according to God?

_____

_____

3. What is God's solution for backslidden Laodicean Christians?

_____

_____

4. What do the following refer to that God counsels Laodicean Christians to buy from Him?
   Gold _____

   White Raiment _____

   Eye Salve _____

Prayer Activity

- Call your prayer partner and discuss this devotional with him/her.
- Pray with your prayer partner:
    1. for God to baptize you with His Holy Spirit.
    2. for God to give you the desire to commit 100 percent to Him.
    3. for God to give you the gold, white raiment, and eye salve.
    4. for God to revive you and His church.
    5. for those on your prayer list.

Day 8

Nature's Illustration

An important lesson to learn as Christians is to wait on God, which means resting in entire dependence on Him for everything. We can learn how to wait on God by observing nature. God provides for the animals, and they must wait on Him to provide.

"These [animals] all wait for You, that You may give them their food in due season. What You give them they gather in; You open Your hand, they are filled with good" (Ps. 104:27, 28).

It was God's work to create, and it is God's work to maintain His creation. The Bible tells us that God is "upholding all things by the word of His power" (Heb. 1:3). That is how He established all things, and that is how He wants us to view Him—as our maintainer and provider. God intimately desires to be connected to His creation—to you and me.

Jesus used nature as an illustration of our need to wait for God to provide. He promises us that we do not need to worry with Him in charge:

"Therefore I say to you, do not worry about your life, what you will eat or what you will drink; nor about your body, what you will put on. Is not life more than food and the body more than clothing? Look at the birds of the air, for they neither sow nor reap nor gather into barns; yet your heavenly Father feeds them. Are you not of more value than they? Which of you by worrying can add one cubit to his stature? So why do you worry about clothing? Consider the lilies of the field, how they grow: they neither toil nor spin; and yet I say to you that even Solomon in all his glory was not arrayed like one of these. Now if God so clothes the grass of the field, which today is, and tomorrow is thrown into the oven, will He not much more clothe you, O

you of little faith? Therefore do not worry, saying, 'What shall we eat?' or 'What shall we drink?' or 'What shall we wear?' For after all these things the Gentiles seek. For your heavenly Father knows that you need all these things. But seek first the kingdom of God and His righteousness, and all these things shall be added to you. Therefore do not worry about tomorrow, for tomorrow will worry about its own things. Sufficient for the day is its own trouble" (Matt. 6:25-34).

So what is our job; what are we supposed to do? We are to develop an intimate relationship with God, seeking His kingdom and righteousness. If we do this, we have no need to worry about anything. He has promised to provide whatever is needed. We are to live one day at a time and not worry about tomorrow. We are to "wait on God," resting in entire dependence on Him.

Also, notice what Jesus said in the verse before this section of the Sermon on the Mount:

"No one can serve two masters; for either he will hate the one and love the other, or else he will be loyal to the one and despise the other. You cannot serve God and mammon" (Matt. 6:24).

The next verse begins with the word "therefore." The word "therefore" indicates the coming statement is related to the statement before it. Hence, Jesus is saying that we are serving "mammon" or the god of money if we worry about the necessities of life. When we worry about the necessities of life, we are actually focusing on money and material things rather than God. That is why Jesus said when we do that we are "serving mammon" or worshipping mammon. Therefore, learning to wait on God to provide for our needs is actually a matter of worship.

Personal Reflection and Discussion

1. What does the phrase "waiting on God" mean?

_____

_____

2. What has God given us to illustrate what it means to wait on God?

_____

_____

3. How does nature reveal the truth about waiting on God?

_____

_____

4. What attitude should Christians have concerning their needs being met?

_____

_____

5. If we are worried about our needs being met, what are we actually doing in relation to worship?

_____

_____

Prayer Activity

- **Call your prayer partner and discuss this devotional with him/her.**
- **Pray with your prayer partner:**
    1. **for God to baptize you with His Holy Spirit.**
    2. **for God to revive you and His church.**
    3. **for God to give you the faith to believe that He will provide for all your needs.**
    4. **for God to help you not to worry about anything.**
    5. **for the individuals on your prayer list.**

Our relationship with God is centered on our ability to wait on Him, depending on Him 100 percent for everything. If we lack the faith to wait on God, then we don't really know Him or we don't understand how this area fits into our lives as Christians.

Concerning the first reason—lack of knowing God—if we knew God better we would not be concerned about anything: personal problems, work problems, the necessities of life, church problems, world issues, etc.

David wrote: "Truly my soul silently waits for God; from Him comes my salvation" (Ps. 62:1).

The Hebrew word translated "salvation" in this verse refers to deliverance from threat. Salvation means that God will provide for all our needs: personal, physical, emotional, and spiritual. There are many promises that tell us about God's providence: "Oh, taste and see that the Lord *is* good; blessed is the man who trusts in Him! Oh, fear the Lord, you His saints! There is no want to those who fear Him" (Ps. 34:8, 9).

"And my God shall supply all your need according to His riches in glory by Christ Jesus" (Phil. 4:19).

God's covenant promise to His people contains three things He promises to provide for His children. We read of these in John's third letter. "Beloved, I pray that you may prosper in all things and be in health, just as your soul prospers" (3 John 2).

God promises spiritual prosperity (eternal life), health (physical and emotional), and material prosperity. Of course, there are conditions for these to be fulfilled. The material prosperity mentioned here does not mean that God will make us rich. In fact, we are warned not to seek material riches: "But those who desire to be rich fall into temptation and a snare, and into many foolish and harmful lusts which drown men in destruction and perdition" (1 Tim. 6:9). Instead, God will provide for our material needs. We should not worry about this aspect of our lives. In actuality God desires to provide us with more than we need materially so that we can be a blessing to others by sharing from the abundance God has given us.

When we worry about whether or not the Lord will provide for our needs, we are acting like children who distrust their parents to provide. How would you feel if your young daughter asked you, "Daddy, are you going to feed me tomorrow?"

How would you reply? I am sure you would say, "I love you. Of course I am going to feed you tomorrow."

But what if she asked you the next day, "Daddy, are you going to feed me tomorrow?" How would you feel? And how would you feel if she kept asking this question every day?

This is how we treat God when we worry about the necessities of life. Such anxiety indicates that we really don't trust Him or believe He loves us and will provide for us as He has promised.

I believe that 3 John 2 also seems to indicate that our material and health prosperity is dependent on our "soul" or spiritual prosperity. Our spiritual prosperity is dependent on our relationship with God. So, the more intimately we know God and understand His will, the more these promises will be fulfilled in our lives, and the more we will patiently wait in faith on Him to provide. This relationship between our spiritual prosperity and material prosperity is also taught when Jesus said, "Seek ye first the kingdom of God, and his righteousness; and all these things shall be added unto you" (Matt. 6:33).

Personal Reflection and Discussion

1. Do you find it difficult to wait on God? Why, or why not?

_____
_____

2. List two Bible promises where God promises to provide for your needs.

_____
_____

3. In God's covenant what three things does He promise to His people? How does it make you feel to know that He wants to give you these good things?

_____
_____

4. When we worry about our needs being met, what are we really saying about God?

_____
_____

5. What areas in your life do you worry about the most? What can you do to turn these worries over to God?

_____
_____

Prayer Activity

- Call your prayer partner and discuss this devotional with him/her.
- Pray with your prayer partner:
    1. for God to baptize you with His Holy Spirit.
    2. for God to revive you and His church.
    3. for God to forgive you for distrusting Him.
    4. for God to give you the faith to trust Him to provide for you.
    5. for the individuals on your prayer list.

Man Created to Wait on God

Man was created to be a vessel to be used by God. Through man, God can manifest His power and goodness on this earth. Man does not contain power or goodness by himself—he is completely dependent on His heavenly Father.

We were created to be dependent on God for all things. Yet, because we do not realize our absolute helplessness, we do not see more of God's power in our lives. We tend to have no sense of our need for absolute and unceasing dependence on God in *everything*. God pointed out this problem of independence in His message to the last church living on earth—the Laodicean church:

"Because you say, 'I am rich, have become wealthy, and have need of nothing'—and do not know that you are wretched, miserable, poor, blind, and naked" (Rev. 3:17).

God wants to impart to us everything we need:

"But of Him you are in Christ Jesus, who became for us wisdom from God—and righteousness and sanctification and redemption—that, as it is written, 'He who glories, let him glory in the Lord' " (1 Cor. 1:30, 31).

He wants to give us His nature, character, life, strength, and wisdom. However, the daily baptism of the Holy Spirit is necessary for this to happen. Why? Because, it is through the baptism of the Holy Spirit that Jesus lives in us, and it is through Jesus that we have all these things that God wants to provide for us.

We limit God by our indifference, impatience, and self-effort. In making life's decisions, we often impetuously decide without even asking or waiting for God to reveal His will to us. Not only do we make our own decisions about life, but we also decide where we want to serve God and how we want to do it rather than asking God to reveal to us where He can use us most effectively for His glory.

When we are close to God and have learned to wait on Him, He will guide us in service for Him. If we don't learn the lesson of waiting on God, we will find that much of what we have done has been motivated by our own thoughts and plans, not God's. If we have done this, then in the end we will discover too late that much of what we have done has come to naught:

"Now if anyone builds on this foundation with gold, silver, precious stones, wood, hay, straw, each one's work will become clear; for the Day will declare it, because it will be revealed by fire; and the fire will test each one's work, of what sort it is. If anyone's work which he has built on it endures, he will receive a reward. If anyone's work is burned, he will suffer loss; but he himself will be saved, yet so as through fire" (1 Cor. 3:12-15).

Waiting on God does not come naturally. From childhood onward we learn that we must "do" for ourselves if we are to achieve our goals. At least in the Western world we are taught that we are to be independent and self-sufficient.

With God it is just the opposite. We are to look to God for all things. This doesn't mean that effort is not involved. Once we know God's will, it will take effort and sacrifice to carry out the mission He has given us. Yet even in this we are to be dependent on God for wisdom, guidance, and strength.

For the Christian to have this kind of relationship with God, he must daily spend time with God through prayer and Bible study. He must maintain a moment-by-moment communion:

"Pray without ceasing" (1 Thess. 5:17).

Personal Reflection and Discussion

1. Why do Christians not see more of God's power in their lives?

_____

_____

2. How much of what we need does God desire to impart to us?

_____

_____

3. In what ways do we limit God in our life and service for Him?

_____

_____

4. If we are serving God with our own plans and methods, what will be the outcome of our efforts? Have you experienced this type of outcome before?

_____

_____

Prayer Activity

- Call your prayer partner and discuss this devotional with him/her.
- Pray with your prayer partner:
    1. for God to baptize you with His Holy Spirit.
    2. for God to revive you and His church.
    3. for God to forgive you for not depending on Him as He desires you to.
    4. for God to lead you to look to Him for all things in life and service.
    5. for the individuals on your prayer list.

The True
Expression of Our Faith

The same principle of waiting on God applies to our struggles with temptation and sin. We are 100 percent dependent on Jesus for victory over these areas of our life. Waiting on God is a major factor in the victories we have over Satan.

Jesus lives in the Christian through the baptism of the Holy Spirit. Therefore, we have every virtue of Jesus—His love, joy, peace, faith, patience, pure thoughts, etc.—in us because Jesus is living in us. So when we are tempted, we are simply to look to Jesus for deliverance from the temptation. We are to wait on Jesus for the victory.

"Let us lay aside every weight, and the sin which so easily ensnares us, and let us run with endurance the race that is set before us, looking unto Jesus, the author and finisher of our faith" (Heb. 12:1, 2).

Referring to those who find the Christian life discouraging, Andrew Murray, the well-known Christian author of a past generation, wrote: "Dear soul! How little they know that the abiding in Christ is just meant for the weak, and so beautifully suited for their feebleness. It is not the doing of some great thing, and does not demand that we first lead a very holy and devoted life. No, it is simply weakness entrusting itself to a Mighty One to be kept—the unfaithful one casting self on One who is altogether trustworthy and true. Abiding in Him is not a work that we have to do as the condition for enjoying His salvation, but a consenting to let Him do all for us, and in us, and through us. It is a work He does for us—the fruit and the power of His redeeming love. Our part is simply to yield, to trust, and to wait for what He has engaged to perform" (*Abiding in Christ*, p. 23).

Biblical waiting on God is the only true expression of our faith in God. It is the true revelation of our relationship with God. If we truly wait on God, we will never be worried or anxious about anything and never make an impetuous decision, we will have a deep peace in our heart and a calm trustful demeanor, and we will be constantly looking to Jesus for victory over temptation.

How can this be our experience? We must trust God's promise to always provide for us in everything and believe that He will never disappoint us.

"My soul, wait silently for God alone, for my expectation is from Him. He only is my rock and my salvation; He is my defense; I shall not be moved. In God is my salvation and my glory; the rock of my strength, And my refuge, is in God. Trust in Him at all times, you people; pour out your heart before Him; God is a refuge for us" (Ps. 62:5-8).

Those ready to meet Jesus will have learned how to wait on God. I pray that the Lord will use these devotional studies to prepare the last generation for the "waiting" that will be required in order to be ready for Christ's return, because just before Jesus returns God's people will be thrown into the most difficult time they have ever faced—the time of trouble or tribulation. At that time in earth's history they will only have God to look to for their daily provision and protection. If they have learned to wait on God, they will be prepared for this challenging time.

Of course, our victory is sure. When Christ returns "He will swallow up death forever, And the Lord God will wipe away tears from all faces; the rebuke of His people He will take away from all the earth; For the Lord has spoken" (Isa. 25:8).

Personal Reflection and Discussion

1. When Jesus lives in us, which of His qualities do we have?

_____

_____

2. How does the "waiting on God" principle apply to overcoming temptation and sin?

_____

_____

3. How is our waiting on God the true revelation of our faith in God?

_____

_____

4. How can waiting on God become our daily experience?

_____

_____

5. Why is waiting on God important as we approach the last days of earth's history? Are you personally ready for the time of trouble?

_____

_____

Prayer Activity

- **Call your prayer partner and discuss this devotional with him/her.**
- **Pray with your prayer partner:**
    1. **for God to baptize you with His Holy Spirit.**
    2. **for God to revive you and His church.**
    3. **for God to teach you how to wait on Him for everything.**
    4. **for the individuals on your prayer list.**

Waiting for the Manifestation of Christ

Two thousand years ago Israel waited for the manifestation of Christ. We are told that Simeon, a just and devout man, and Anna, a prophetess, both looked for Christ to appear in Israel. Though Simeon and Anna longed for Christ to be manifest in Israel, they could do nothing to make it happen. They had to wait in faith and depend on God for the promise to come to fruition.

The angel came to Mary and told her that Jesus would be brought forth through her: "And behold, you will conceive in your womb and bring forth a Son, and shall call His name Jesus" (Luke 1:31). This was not to happen by her will, but by the will of God. Her part was to accept the word of God through the angel and wait in faith for the manifestation of the promise—the birth of Christ. There was nothing she could do to make it happen except wait and believe.

So it is with us. It is by waiting on God in faith to work in us and through us that Christ is manifest in us today. God did not send His Son to this earth to die for our sins and save us and then leave us to figure things out on our own and make salvation happen within us.

"For by grace you have been saved through faith, and that not of yourselves; it is the gift of God, not of works, lest anyone should boast. For **we are his workmanship**, created in Christ Jesus for good works, which God prepared beforehand that we should walk in them" (Eph. 2:8-10, emphasis added).

Christ was manifested in this world by the power of the Holy Spirit: "And the angel answered and said to her, 'The Holy Spirit will come upon you, and the power of the Highest will overshadow you; therefore, also, that Holy One who is to be born will be called the Son of God'" (Luke 1:35).

So also, Christ is to be manifest in and through us by the power of the Holy Spirit. The angel brought to Mary the opportunity of Christ being manifest to the world through her. Her part was to choose to let it happen and wait for the full manifestation to take place—in her case nine months.

The same is true of us. The New Testament teaches that Christ lives in the believer through the Holy Spirit. It is through receiving the daily baptism of the Holy Spirit that Jesus lives or abides in us. It is through Spirit baptism that He ministers in and through us, and manifests His righteousness through us.

The New Testament is very clear about the necessity of Christ living in us in order for us to have victory over temptation and sin—His righteousness manifest in our lives. Jesus used the imagery of the vine and branches to illustrate this truth:

"Abide in me, and I in you. As the branch cannot bear fruit of itself, unless it abides in the vine, neither can you, unless you abide in Me. 'I am the vine, you are the branches. He who abides in Me, and I in him, bears much fruit; for without Me you can do nothing'" (John 15:4, 5).

Paul taught this truth throughout his writings:

"Likewise you also, reckon yourselves to be dead indeed to sin, but alive to God in Christ Jesus our Lord" (Rom. 6:11).

"We have the mind of Christ" (1 Cor. 2:16).

If we choose to receive the baptism of the Holy Spirit and wait in faith for Christ to fill us, then He will be manifest in us His wisdom, His righteousness, His sanctification, and His redemption: "But of Him you are in Christ Jesus, who became for us wisdom from

God—and righteousness and sanctification and redemption" (1 Cor. 1:30).

Waiting on God for Christ to be manifest in us and for victory over temptation is the same as waiting on God for every other provision in life. God wants us to look to Him for victory. Of this Ellen White wrote:

"When His words of instruction have been received, and have taken possession of us, Jesus is to us an abiding presence, controlling our thoughts, and ideas and actions. . . . It is no more we that live, but Christ that liveth in us, and He is the hope of glory. Self is dead, but Christ is a living Saviour" (*Testimonies to Ministers and Gospel Workers*, p. 389).

Do you see the beauty of this truth? Our part is to wait in trusting faith, believing God's promise to manifest Christ and His righteousness in us. Our only part is to choose to let this happen and believe it will happen, just as Mary did. When unrighteous desires and temptations come, we are not to fight against them. We are to turn to Christ who is living within us and ask Him to manifest His own righteousness: "Looking unto Jesus, the author and finisher of our faith" (Heb. 12:2). Then we are to wait in faith, believing He will do it.

Personal Reflection and Discussion

1. Could Simeon, Anna, or Mary do anything to make the manifestation of Christ happen?

_____

_____

2. Describe in your own words how Christ is to be manifest in you today.

_____

_____

3. When you are tempted, how are you to obtain the victory?

_____

_____

Prayer Activity

● **Call your prayer partner and discuss this devotional with him/her.**
● **Pray with your prayer partner:**
   1. for God to baptize you with His Holy Spirit.
   2. for God to revive you and His church.
   3. for God to manifest Christ in your life today.
   4. for Jesus to give you His victory when you are tempted to sin.
   5. for the individuals on your prayer list.

Day 13

Hearing God's Word for Guidance

We have been given the Word of God as a set of instructions to guide us through life. David was well aware of God's Word and referred to it often in the psalms he wrote. Yet in the twenty-fifth psalm, he asked:

"Show me Your ways, O Lord; Teach me Your paths. Lead me in Your truth and teach me, for You are the God of my salvation; on You I wait all the day" (Ps. 25:4, 5).

Even though David had the Word of God, he realized that he needed God's instruction concerning its application in His life and the service God had called him to perform. Therefore, he asked God for His revelation.

Revelation and information are two different things. God's Word contains a wealth of information; however, knowing this information is not enough. We need to "hear" God's application of His Word in our life. When we "hear" God's instruction, it becomes a revelation of His will and our faith is increased, which strengthens us to carry out His will. That is why Paul wrote:

"So then faith comes by **hearing**, and **hearing** by the word of God" (Rom. 10:17, emphasis added).

I will share an experience from my early ministry to illustrate this point. I had been working at my first church assignment after graduating from seminary for about six months when I decided to conduct an evangelistic series. The plans were laid and everything was in place. But one morning, while sitting in the church office, I began feeling a little fearful. This was the first evangelistic meeting I had conducted, and it seemed somewhat overwhelming. I didn't know what was going to happen. Was anyone going to come? Would everything go OK? Would there be any decisions for Christ? As these anxious feelings engulfed me, I knelt down and talked to the Lord about the situation. During the prayer I was impressed to read the Bible, so I got up and opened the Bible to the book of John. As I read I came to John 15:16:

"You did not choose Me, but I chose you and appointed you that you should go and bear fruit, and that your fruit should remain, that whatever you ask the Father in My name He may give you."

As I silently read this verse, it seemed to sound audibly in my ears. It was as though God spoke it to me. I heard God's Word to me. My faith was strengthened, and I was encouraged that the meetings would go well, and they did.

That was the first experience I recall of waiting on God to hear His instruction for me in a particular situation. Of course, He had directed me many times before. But I was young and just learning how the Lord leads His children.

God wants to direct all His children in the way that they should go, in the decisions they should make. Our part is to humbly seek His guidance and wait until His will becomes clear. He will always hear and answer such prayers.

"I will instruct you and teach you in the way you should go: I will guide you with My eye" (Ps. 32:8).

Personal Reflection and Discussion

1. What is the difference between receiving information and receiving revelation from God's Word?
_____
_____

2. What must we do in order to receive God's guidance?
_____
_____

3. List one or more scriptures where God promises to guide His children.
_____
_____

4. Give one or more examples when you have received a revelation from God's Word that has guided your life.
_____
_____

Prayer Activity

- Call your prayer partner and discuss this devotional with him/her.
- Pray with your prayer partner:
    1. for God to baptize you with His Holy Spirit.
    2. for God to revive you and His church.
    3. for God to guide you in every detail of your life.
    4. for the individuals on your prayer list.

Revelation vs. Human Logic for Guidance

There are two things we must know in order to receive God's guidance. First, we must realize that we absolutely need it. Second, we must wait on God for His guidance. We must never make decisions using our own reasoning and logic. For example, when Jesus gave the disciples the great gospel commission, He told them, "'Go therefore and make disciples of all the nations, baptizing them in the name of the Father and of the Son and of the Holy Spirit, teaching them to observe all things that I have commanded you; and lo, I am with you always, even to the end of the age.' Amen" (Matt. 28:19, 20).

Normal human logic or "logic of the flesh" would conclude that the gospel should be preached in every village the disciples passed through. However, this was not the case. The disciples needed God's direction to know when and where He wanted them to preach. They were to wait on Him until that direction came. They were not to go forward preaching the gospel until they had clear revelation from God as to where to go.

We see this illustrated in Paul's missionary journey described in the book of Acts:

"Now when they had gone through Phrygia and the region of Galatia, they were forbidden by the Holy Spirit to preach the word in Asia. After they had come to Mysia, they tried to go into Bithynia, but the Spirit did not permit them. So passing by Mysia, they came down to Troas. And a vision appeared to Paul in the night. A man of Macedonia stood and pleaded with him, saying, 'Come over to Macedonia and help us.' Now after he had seen the vision, immediately we sought to go to Macedonia, concluding that the Lord had called us to preach the gospel to them" (Acts 16:6-10).

They were going to go to Asia, but the Spirit said no. Then they were going to preach the gospel in Mysia and Bithynia, but the Spirit said no again. Then the Spirit gave Paul a vision indicating they should go to Macedonia. Immediately, they followed the Spirit's direction and preached the gospel there.

As the disciples did, we must also learn to wait on God's direction and instruction in our personal life and service for him. I have been a pastor for many years, and it is easy for me to think I know what the Lord would have me to do. However, that is a dangerous position for me to take. I am an apprentice shepherd working for Christ, the great Shepherd. I am to follow His directions as pastor and not simply do what I think should be done. This requires learning how to wait on the Lord for guidance. That is what David said he did:

"Lead me in Your truth and teach me, For you are the God of my salvation; on You I wait all the day" (Ps. 25:5).

A well-known proverb supports this biblical teaching:

"Trust in the Lord with all your heart; and lean not on your own understanding; in all your ways acknowledge Him, and He shall direct your paths" (Prov. 3:5, 6).

This text clearly teaches that we are not to lean or depend on our own understanding. Instead, we are to trust God for guidance by "acknowledging" Him, which means by keeping an intimate moment-by-moment connection with Him. We are to constantly wait on God, looking to Him to direct all our paths in life, not just our spiritual path.

Often, I remind myself that I don't know how to pastor, even though I have 30–plus years in full-time ministry, most of that as a pastor. For me, this helps me keep my focus on the Lord. I must continually look to Him for guidance in the ministry He wants to perform through me. All leaders in God's church are in danger of forgetting who they work for. The more experience we have and the higher up in the organization we go, the greater danger we are in of following our own thoughts and our own ideas in carrying out God's work. Our prayer for guidance can become a ceremonial duty before we begin our day or a meeting rather than an earnest seeking of God's guidance.

Personal Reflection and Discussion

1. What two things must we know in order to receive God's guidance?

_____

_____

2. Is it safe to follow human logic when seeking to follow God's instruction? Why, or why not?

_____

_____

3. Give a biblical illustration where human logic would have led the disciples to incorrectly follow God's instruction.

_____

_____

4. What is one of our great dangers when we have been in God's work for many years? How do we avoid this danger?

_____

_____

Prayer Activity

● Call your prayer partner and discuss this devotional with him/her.
● Pray with your prayer partner:
    1. for God to baptize you with His Holy Spirit.
    2. for God to revive you and His church.
    3. for God to teach you to wait for His guidance.
    4. for the individuals on your prayer list.

Decisions in the Spirit or in the Flesh

When we begin doing what we think should be done in our life and God's work without waiting for God's direction, we are working in the flesh using our own strength and wisdom. We must realize that we can accomplish nothing of real value unless God works in and through us. This is why Paul writes in 1 Corinthians 1:30: "But of Him you are in Christ Jesus, who became for us wisdom from God."

Therefore, when we pray we must express to God our sense of need and our faith in His willingness to instruct and guide us. Pride and self–assurance will get in the way of this happening. Only the "meek" will receive such guidance from the Lord. David stated this in the following way: "The humble He guides in justice, and the humble He teaches His way" (Ps. 25:9).

You see, it requires meekness, humility, and a trusting faith to wait on God for His guidance and not rush headlong in the direction we think we should go. And when we have meekly asked for His guidance, we must then continue looking to God "all day" for the guidance He has promised. Therefore, we will be continually waiting on the Lord for guidance. As we wait on God for guidance, we are acknowledging that He is the only source of wisdom. We are acknowledging our complete dependence on Him for direction in our personal life and service for Him. This type of waiting provides us with a sense of peace and hope.

Of course, even if we learn to humbly wait on the Lord, we are in constant danger as Christians of reverting back to the flesh and relying on ourselves. This happened many times in the Bible. In Psalm 106 the history of the nation of Israel is remembered. Unfortunately, these sad words are recorded: "They soon forgot His works; they did not wait for His counsel" (Ps. 106:13).

We know the sad history of what happened to Israel when they stopped waiting for God's guidance. They began following their own ways, which led away from God and led to destruction. Over and over again we read of God's people choosing to follow their own ways and not wait for God's direction. Each time led to serious consequences. We see this when Joshua led Israel against Ai, when they made a covenant with the Gibeonites, and when Israel did not follow God's direction when they entered the Promised Land.

We are all in danger of doing the same thing. We have God's Word. We think we know how it applies to us, and we move forward in a certain application without waiting on the Lord for direction. As Adventists we see this repeated time and again when the Sabbath truth is shared with someone who thinks they "know" the Word of God. After hearing about the Sabbath, many of these individuals continue to keep Sunday instead of the seventh-day Sabbath because they make their decision based on what they think God would have them do, instead of waiting for His direction in their life.

We must be careful not to become boastful as we talk about people who haven't accepted the Sabbath truth. How many times have we made personal decisions in the same manner which prove to be disastrous? How many times have we made decisions about God's work and later it proved not to have God's blessing? We are in constant danger when we attend committee or board meetings, prayer meetings, or worship services and assume that we know the will of God because we have His Word, previous experience, and our traditions. We believe that because we have these things we will come to the right conclusion concerning the will of God on some personal or church matter. However, there may be insights in God's Word we don't have and experiences we are lacking. Unless we wait on God for His wisdom and guidance, we will be led by the flesh and find ourselves out of the will of God. How true the text is that says "There is a way that seems right to a man, but its end is the way of death" (Prov. 16:25).

Why do we make decisions and not wait on God? Remember, "Pride goes before destruction, and a haughty spirit before a fall" (Prov. 16:18).

Personal Reflection and Discussion

1. What does it mean to serve God in the flesh? Do you struggle with this?

_____

_____

2. How can we avoid serving God in the flesh?

_____

_____

3. What are the requirements to receive God's guidance?

_____

_____

4. Why do Christians often make wrong decisions thinking they are following the Lord's will?

_____

_____

Prayer Activity

- **Call your prayer partner and discuss this devotional with him/her.**
- **Pray with your prayer partner:**
    1. **for God to baptize you with His Holy Spirit.**
    2. **for God to revive you and His church.**
    3. **for God to help you avoid serving Him in the flesh.**
    4. **for the individuals on your prayer list.**

Waiting on God in Prayer

When we pray we are usually asking God to provide for some material, emotional, spiritual, or physical need. It is natural and easy to become anxious and not wait in quietness for the fulfillment of our prayer request. At such times we can become impatient. However, we must learn to wait on God in prayer.

True waiting on God in prayer is not limited to persevering in prayer in order to get what we desire or what God has promised. The element of waiting on God in restful faith is certainly an important part of persevering prayer. However, true waiting in prayer is something much deeper. It is something related to deepening one's relationship with God, not simply waiting for Him to give us the things we are praying for.

New Christians mainly set their hearts on seeking the blessings and gifts God promises to give if they pray for them. God uses the basic needs we long for and pray about to draw us closer to Him. His desire is to give Himself to us so we can experience Him and His goodness. Often He withholds giving us what we ask for in order to draw us closer to Him.

When this happens, our waiting in prayer becomes a worship experience with God. We begin focusing more and more on His goodness, and we grow in trusting His faithfulness. When we begin experiencing such deep encounters with God Himself during our waiting times in prayer, we will begin to desire more time in waiting day by day. Our prayer times will become less and less motivated by our needs, and more and more motivated to wait with God in prayer in order to experience Him. Then we begin to experience the idea of praying without ceasing, which Paul referred to in 1 Thessalonians 5:17. Thus, we will also develop within us the ability to "rejoice always" (1 Thess. 5:16).

In this process of waiting with God in prayer, we will develop the attitude of waiting on God as we go about our daily activities. We will grow in our utter dependence on Him in everything, and we will seek to be intimately connected with God on a daily basis. With this continual dependence comes deep peace of heart and mind. All worry and anxiety are dissolved and the present or future do not concern us or cause us stress.

This kind of waiting on God in prayer takes time to develop. Many things can get in the way of our waiting time with God. We can study and read the teachings of Christian authors to the neglect of true waiting on God. We can allow our work or our ministry to separate us from the intimate relationship with Him such waiting brings.

"The Lord is good to those who wait for Him" (Lam. 3:25).

When we wait on God in this manner, we experience His goodness—we experience God Himself. This kind of experience with God comes only by waiting on Him in prayer. It is also an essential element of coming to know God intimately, which is at the heart of our salvation relationship with Him.

"And this is eternal life, that they may know You, the only true God, and Jesus Christ whom You have sent" (John 17:3).

The more we develop this kind of relationship with God, the more unshakeable we will become in our faith and faithfulness to God. Also, we will experience more quietness and deep peace in our soul. Anxiety, worry, and fear will be gone. This experience will bring us great strength in the Lord, which is necessary for all to have who are ready to meet Jesus when He returns.

Personal Reflection and Discussion

1. What does it mean to wait on God in prayer?

_____

_____

2. What is God's purpose in delaying an answer to our prayer?

_____

_____

3. What does waiting on God in prayer do for our relationship with God?

_____

_____

4. Why must those who are ready to meet Jesus learn to wait on God in prayer?

_____

_____

Prayer Activity

- Call your prayer partner and discuss this devotional with him/her.
- Pray with your prayer partner:
    1. for God to baptize you with His Holy Spirit.
    2. for God to revive you and His church.
    3. for God to teach you how to wait on Him in prayer.
    4. for the individuals on your prayer list.

Day 17

God's Sovereignty Over All Things

Waiting on God refers to the Christian's ability to maintain a confident, quiet, expectant, hopeful, peaceful trust in God at all times for all things. In order for believers to be able to wait on God in this manner, they must understand God's sovereignty. The Christian must believe that God is a sovereign ruler and is able to do what He promises. If God is not sovereign, then Satan can keep God from carrying out His promises to those who believe His Word.

God's sovereignty refers to His lordship or rulership in this world. The Bible clearly states that at the cross Satan's power was broken and Christ was "declared to be the Son of God with power, according to the Spirit of holiness, by the resurrection from the dead" (Rom. 1:4). And Jesus stated of Himself after His resurrection: "Then Jesus came and spoke to them saying, 'All authority has been given to Me in heaven and on earth'" (Matt. 28:18).

Paul wrote of Christ's exaltation and authority in his letter to the Ephesians. He wrote that the Father "seated Him at His right hand in the heavenly places, far above all principality and power and might and dominion, and every name that is named, not only in this age but also in that which is to come. And He put all things under His feet, and gave Him to be head over all things to the church, which is His body, the fullness of Him who fills all in all" (Eph. 1:20-23).

When one looks at the events on earth, it is easy to question who is regulating what is happening today—God or Satan. The majority deny God's sovereign rule on earth. Many deny that God created the earth. Few believe that God is concerned with or regulating what He created. Most look to the "laws of nature" or "Mother Nature" as ruling the natural world. The majority of people look to psychology, behavioral science, and sociology to understand man's behavior. Man has made man autonomous. Man has made man lord of human affairs in the world, and Mother Nature is made ruler of the natural world.

When we look at the world and the affairs of men, does it look like God is in control? Doesn't everything indicate that Satan is in more control than God? Don't natural disasters such as hurricanes, earthquakes, tornados, tsunamis, famine, disease, etc., indicate Satan's control? What about man's inhumanity to man? Don't wars, crime, terrorism, etc., indicate Satan's rulership?

I personally believe that the majority of Christians give way too much power to Satan and man. It is almost like some Christians view God as looking down from heaven "wringing His hands" and saying, "I wish man wouldn't do this or that," or "I wish Satan wasn't so effective in carrying out his plans." Dear Christian, we serve the sovereign Ruler of the universe, who is not controlled by His creatures or the laws of nature He created.

Our answer as to whether God or Satan is in control depends on whether we are walking by faith in God's Word, the Bible, or walking by sight, looking to circumstances and conditions in the world.

There are only two alternatives as to who is in control. God must either rule or be ruled. God must either accomplish His own will or be stopped by His creation—the forces of nature and man.

Let's look at what the Bible says about God's sovereignty on earth. Paul tells us that God "works all things according to the counsel of His will" (Eph. 1:11).

All things are subject to God's immediate control. All things happen according to His eternal purpose.

We might reason, "If I were God, I wouldn't allow this or that to happen!" At such times we must remember what Paul told the believers in Rome:

"Oh, the depth of the riches both of the wisdom and knowledge of God! How unsearchable are His judgments and His ways past finding out!" (Rom. 11:33).

Sovereignty characterizes the whole being of God. He is sovereign in the exercise of His power, and His power is exercised as He wills, when He wills, and where He wills.

Personal Reflection and Discussion

1. Why is a belief in God's sovereignty essential in order to wait on Him?

_____

_____

2. What happened to Satan's power and authority at the cross of Christ? Why is this important in understanding God's sovereignty?

_____

_____

3. What position of authority did Christ receive after His death and resurrection?

_____

_____

4. The Bible says that God works all things according to the _____ of His _____. What does this mean to you?

_____

_____

Prayer Activity

- Call your prayer partner and discuss this devotional with him/her.
- Pray with your prayer partner:
    1. for God to baptize you with His Holy Spirit.
    2. for God to revive you and His church.
    3. for God to teach you that He is the sovereign ruler in heaven and earth.
    4. for the individuals on your prayer list.

God's Sovereignty Over Nature

The Bible clearly teaches that God rules over nature. There is no part of nature that is out of His control. The psalmist wrote:

"For I know that the Lord is great, and our Lord is above all gods. Whatever the Lord pleases He does, in heaven and in earth, in the seas and in all deep places. He causes the vapors to ascend from the ends of the earth; He makes lightning for the rain; He brings the wind out of His treasuries" (Ps. 135:5-7).

One might ask, "Isn't Satan involved in nature's destructive force?" The answer is yes. However, Satan can rule in nature only to the extent that the Lord allows. Satan can influence nature only to the extent that his activities carry out God's eternal purpose. This has to be the case or Paul's statement in Romans would not be true:

"And we know that all things work together for good to those who love God, to those who are the called according to His purpose" (Rom. 8:28).

If God did not reign as sovereign Lord over nature and man, this promise would not always be true for the believer. Satan would see to it that many things would not work out for their good. He would work all things for their destruction.

We clearly see the sovereignty of God over Satan's efforts to destroy Job. God gave Satan permission to bring severe trials upon Job; however, God limited what Satan could do:

"So the Lord said to Satan, 'Behold, all that he has is in your power; only do not lay a hand on his person.' Then Satan went out from the presence of the Lord" (Job 1:12).

In the verses that follow, we read that Satan was allowed to take Job's possessions and children. Here we clearly see that Satan can control nature only to the degree God allows.

Over and over again in the Old Testament we see God in control of nature.

- Genesis 6:17 – the Flood
- Genesis 6:19, 20 – the animals that entered the ark
- Exodus 8-10 – the plagues of Egypt: frogs, flies, thunder, hail, fire, darkness
- Joshua 10:12, 13 – the sun and moon stood still
- Isaiah 38:1-8 – the sun moved back 10 degrees
- 1 Kings 17:2-4 – ravens fed Elijah
- Jonah 1:17 – a large fish saved Jonah
- Daniel 3:25-27 – three Hebrews saved from the fiery furnace
- Daniel 6:22 – lions kept from killing Daniel

Jesus Christ was God in the flesh: "In the beginning was the Word, and the Word was with God, and the Word was God. . . . And the Word became flesh and dwelt among us, and we beheld His glory, the glory as of the only begotten of the Father, full of grace and truth" (John 1:1, 14). Therefore, we also see God's sovereignty over nature in the New Testament manifested through Jesus.

- Mark 4:36-41 – a storm quieted
- Mark 6:35-44 –the loaves and fishes multiplied to feed more than 5,000 people
- Mark 6:45-51 – Jesus and Peter walked on water
- Matthew 17:27 – a fish carried a coin to Peter for taxes
- Matthew 21:18-20 –the fig tree cursed and it died

Because of God's sovereign reign over this earth, we can be assured that God can do and will do what He promises and that Satan cannot stop Him from fulfilling all His promises to those who believe in Him.

Personal Reflection and Discussion

1. How much of the natural world does God have rulership over?

_____

_____

2. Why is it important for Christians to know that God has sovereign rulership over nature?

_____

_____

3. Give examples from the Old Testament of God's sovereign rulership over nature.

_____

_____

4. Give examples from the New Testament of Christ's sovereign rulership over nature.

_____

_____

Prayer Activity

- **Call your prayer partner and discuss this devotional with him/her.**
- **Pray with your prayer partner:**
    1. **for God to baptize you with His Holy Spirit.**
    2. **for God to revive you and His church.**
    3. **for God to help you accept His sovereign rulership over all of nature.**
    4. **for the individuals on your prayer list.**

God's Sovereignty Over Man

One might say, "Well, yes, God may be sovereign over nature, but man has free will." Yes, that is true, but that doesn't negate the fact that God is also sovereign over man. I admit this may be difficult to understand. Yet it is what the Bible teaches. All the actions of God's subjects are under His control. This even applies to rebellious men. They don't know it, but they are carrying out the secret decree of our sovereign God.

This is clearly illustrated in the case of the Pharaoh in Egypt who refused to let Israel go in the time of Moses. Sometimes we find in the Bible what I call God's "revealed will" and His "secret will." These two may seem to contradict each other. However, it is important that we remember not to try to judge God by our standards of fairness or what we think is right or wrong. Often we try to make God into our image. Remember what Paul and Isaiah tell us about this subject:

"Oh, the depth of the riches both of the wisdom and knowledge of God! How unsearchable are His judgments and His ways past finding out!" (Rom. 11:33).

"'For my thoughts are not your thoughts, nor are your ways My ways,' says the Lord" (Isa. 55:8).

God was clearly in control during the exodus of Israel out of Egypt. God told Moses to ask Pharaoh to let Israel go. Then God also said that it was not His will for Pharaoh to let Israel go. Why? Because God wanted to reveal His power to the Egyptians and His people. God said:

"And I will harden Pharaoh's heart, and multiply My signs and My wonders in the land of Egypt. But Pharaoh will not heed you, so that I may lay My hand on Egypt and bring My armies and My people, the children of Israel, out of the land of Egypt by great judgments. And the Egyptians shall know that I am the Lord, when I stretch out My hand on Egypt and bring out the children of Israel from among them" (Ex. 7:3-5).

In this passage we see God's revealed will and secret will stated. His revealed will was for Pharaoh to let Israel go. His secret will was that Pharaoh not let Israel go right away.

The Bible indicates that the way God deals with evil men is to either allow them to carry out their evil actions or stop or limit them in order to fulfill His eternal purpose. In Pharaoh's case God allowed him to rebel against His revealed will. However, God limited Pharaoh's rage against Moses and Israel. Proverbs informs us: "A man's heart plans his way, But the Lord directs his steps" (Prov. 16:9).

Pharaoh's evil heart devised plans to stop God from delivering Israel out of Egypt, and in the end he tried to destroy Israel at the Red Sea. However, Israel's sovereign God overruled the ultimate goal of Pharaoh's evil plans, allowing him to carry them out only to a certain extent of his evil plans. The evil plans God allowed him to carry out were used by God to reveal His power and greatness before Egypt and Israel. God knew it was important for Israel to experience God's might and power, and He used Pharaoh to do this.

"There are many plans in a man's heart, Nevertheless the Lord's counsel—that will stand" (Prov. 19:21).

It is essential to know this about God when we are waiting in prayer for the Lord to deliver us from some difficult situation. For example, I have seen many cases when an individual becomes convicted to keep the seventh-day Sabbath, but their boss threatens to fire them if they don't work on God's holy day. In these types of situations it is comforting to know that God is not in heaven "wringing His hands" in worry hoping this young Christian doesn't lose his or her job. What kind of God is that who is unable to deliver His children? No, God is sovereign and can direct the boss's decision. God can either let the evil plan to fire God's faithful child be carried out, or God can overrule and put it in the heart of the boss to keep the employee. How do I know this? Proverbs tells us that "the king's heart is in the hand of the Lord, like the rivers of water; He turns it wherever He wishes" (Prov. 21:1).

Even though we think we know what is best for us at the time, God has a view of the big picture that we do not have. God does allow doors to close when He needs or wants to open other doors. Otherwise, how could He give us an experience that will in the end glorify His name and work out for our good? Therefore, God may allow us to lose a job over the Sabbath issue. But if He does, He has something better planned for us. Such is the case for all His promises to us.

Personal Reflection and Discussion

1. Which is more difficult for you to believe: that God is sovereign over nature or that God is sovereign over man? Why?

_____

_____

2. What evidences has God given us in the Bible that He is sovereign over man?

_____

_____

3. Why is it important that God have sovereign rulership over man?

_____

_____

Prayer Activity

- Call your prayer partner and discuss this devotional with him/her.
- Pray with your prayer partner:
    1. for God to baptize you with His Holy Spirit.
    2. for God to revive you and His church.
    3. for God to help you place your trust in His sovereign rulership over all of mankind.
    4. for the individuals on your prayer list.

Day 20

God's Sovereignty Illustrated

We see God's sovereign rule over man illustrated in the story of Joseph, Jacob's son. Joseph's older brothers hated him and wanted him dead. One day when Joseph came looking for them far from home the wrathful brothers decided to take the opportunity to finally rid themselves of their father's favorite son. At first they were going to kill him. However, God overruled their murderous plans and allowed them to sell him as a slave to a passing caravan. Joseph was taken to Egypt and sold to a good master, Potiphar: "Now Joseph had been taken down to Egypt. And Potiphar, an officer of Pharaoh, captain of the guard, an Egyptian, bought him from the Ishmaelites who had taken him down there" (Gen. 39:1).

God blessed Joseph as he carried out his stewardship responsibilities. Joseph didn't know it, but he was in training for a future time when he would be steward over much more in the nation of Egypt. God is always working in this manner in our lives. He allows experiences to come to us that prepare us to serve Him even more effectively in the future. Many times these events would not be of our choosing. However, our sovereign God knows what is best for our spiritual development and what experiences we need in order to be a greater blessing to others and bring even greater glory to Him. Knowing this enables us to prayerfully wait in peaceful, trusting faith for God to lead us through these difficult times.

Next, God allowed Potiphar's wife to try to seduce Joseph. Fortunately, Joseph chose to be faithful to God and not dishonor his master. So he rejected her advances and told her, "How then can I do this great wickedness, and sin against God?" (Gen. 39:9). Frustrated and enraged by Joseph's refusal, she accused him of trying to force himself on her. As a result, Joseph was put in prison. Once again, Joseph found himself in a very difficult situation for which he had done nothing to deserve. But again, he chose to be faithful to his God even though it would appear that God had been unfaithful to him by allowing this to happen.

Events will also happen in our life that from outward appearances seem to indicate that God has not been faithful in His promise to us. Many things will happen that we simply don't understand—usually God doesn't reveal the reason until later, or we may never know in this life why He allowed such a thing to happen. Here again we see the necessity of understanding God's sovereignty in order to wait patiently on Him during such times.

Now, fast–forward to the end of Joseph's story when he is exalted right next to Pharaoh in power and authority. Seven years of plenty had come followed by seven years of famine just as God had revealed to Joseph. When the famine came, it affected the area where Joseph's father and brothers were living. They heard there was grain in Egypt. So they went there to buy some to bring back to their families. Joseph recognized his brothers, but they did not recognize their brother, who was now this great man of authority in Egypt. After testing them to see if they had changed, Joseph finally revealed himself to them. He reassured them with love and forgiveness in his voice:

"But now, do not therefore be grieved or angry with yourselves because you sold me here; for God sent me before you to preserve life. . . . And God sent me before you to preserve a posterity for you in the earth, and to save your lives by a great deliverance. So now it was not you who sent me here, but God; and He has made me a father to Pharaoh, and lord of all his house, and a ruler throughout all the land of Egypt" (Gen. 45:5-8).

Joseph had gained a marvelous insight into God's sovereignty. He understood that it was God who allowed Joseph's brothers to carry out their hateful plan. It was God who had allowed all the events of the previous years—events both good and bad from man's perspective. Many things happened to Joseph that certainly went against God's revealed will. It was not God's revealed will for Joseph's brothers to treat him in this manner. It was not God's revealed will for Potiphar's wife to try to seduce Joseph and then lie about what had happened. No, but God's secret will was to allow these things to happen and use them to carry out His plans in Joseph's life.

God works in the same manner in the Christian's life today. He doesn't keep bad things from happening. Instead, He uses them for our good, and anything He knows will not work to be a blessing for us He will keep from happening to us. "Surely the wrath of man shall praise thee: the remainder of wrath shalt thou restrain" (Ps. 76:10).

Personal Reflection and Discussion

1. Does God allow only good things to happen to Christians?

_____

_____

2. What happened to Joseph that could have caused him to doubt God's love and guidance in his life?

_____

_____

3. How does knowing God's sovereignty help Christians remain faithful to God when bad things happen to them?

_____

_____

4. What insight about God did Joseph reveal when he spoke to his brothers when they came before him seeking grain during the famine?

_____

_____

Prayer Activity

- Call your prayer partner and discuss this devotional with him/her.
- Pray with your prayer partner:
    1. for God to baptize you with His Holy Spirit.
    2. for God to revive you and His church.
    3. for God to forgive you when you doubt His love and care for you when something bad happens.
    4. for God to help you embrace the promise that all things work together for your good.
    5. for the individuals on your prayer list.

The story of God delivering Israel from Egypt and the story of Joseph reveal how all things work together for good for God's children: "And we know that all things work together for good to those who love God, to those who are the called according to His purpose" (Rom. 8:28). God does not allow evil men to carry out to the fullest their sadistic plans. However, God has the sovereign ability to use the plans of evil men to carry out His eternal purposes. Yet, God will stop man's evil ways when necessary. We see God clearly stating this truth when He told Israel:

"For I will cast out the nations before you and enlarge your borders; neither will any man covet your land when you go up to appear before the Lord your God three times in the year" (Ex. 34:24).

God indicated that He would intervene to prevent Israel's enemies from attacking them when they were following God's instruction to participate in His sacred yearly feasts. This would be a good time for the enemy to attack, but their sovereign God would not allow this to happen—He would overrule any plans of the enemy.

In the story of Christ's birth we see God using Christ's archenemy, Herod, to direct the wise men to Bethlehem. Herod sought the chief priests of Israel and learned that Christ would be born in Bethlehem. Because Herod then "sent them to Bethlehem" (Matt. 2:8), the wise men were able to bring the gifts that Joseph and Mary would need to flee to Egypt with Jesus when Herod ordered all male children ages 2 and under to be killed. The man who plotted to kill Jesus provided for Him.

Knowing God's sovereignty enables us to wait patiently and hopefully when we are under attack by Satan and evil men. Their plans may be to destroy us, but God will turn their plans and cause them to work together for our good. We may not like what is happening, but we can be assured that our sovereign God is in control of the situation. This understanding will enable you to wait on God day by day in calm, faithful trust.

All men are under God's sovereign control. God has a purpose in allowing evil to proceed on earth. God will allow Satan to carry out many evil plans. However, through it all God's people will be tried and strengthened. That is why James could write:

"My brethren, count it all joy when you fall into various trials, knowing that the testing of your faith produces patience. But let patience have its perfect work, that you may be perfect and complete, lacking nothing" (James 1:2-4).

As we learn to wait patiently, faithfully, and hopefully on our sovereign God, we will be developing the very character we must have in order to be ready to meet Jesus when He comes.

The trials God allows us to go through are essential to the development of Christ's character in us. According to John we must become just like Jesus before He comes in order to be ready for that great event: "Beloved, now we are children of God; and it has not yet been revealed what we shall be, but we know that when He is revealed, we shall be like Him, for we shall see Him as He is" (1 John 3:2).

Ellen White wrote the following about the disappointing trials we go through: "In the future life the mysteries that have annoyed and disappointed us will be made plain. We shall see that our seemingly unanswered prayers and disappointed hopes have been among our greatest blessings" (*Ministry of Healing*, p. 474).

Personal Reflection and Discussion

1. What do the biblical stories of God delivering Israel out of Egypt and the events in Joseph's life reveal about God's sovereign rule over men?

_____

_____

2. What does the story of Christ's birth reveal about God's rulership over the enemies of His people?

_____

_____

3. Why does God allow difficulties and trials to come into the Christian's life?

_____

_____

4. What did Ellen White say about the most difficult times in our life?

_____

_____

Prayer Activity

● Call your prayer partner and discuss this devotional with him/her.
● Pray with your prayer partner:
    1. for God to baptize you with His Holy Spirit.
    2. for God to revive you and His church.
    3. for God to help you to believe that even events that seem bad will work out for your good.
    4. for the individuals on your prayer list.

Trying Events and God's Sovereignty

Christians should not be surprised when trials and difficulties come into their lives. Concerning this Peter wrote:

"Beloved, do not think it strange concerning the fiery trial which is to try you, as though some strange thing happened to you; but rejoice to the extent that you partake of Christ's sufferings, that when His glory is revealed, you may also be glad with exceeding joy" (1 Peter 4:12, 13).

God will allow evil men to work against us. We will be lied about, cheated, and treated unfairly. We will face Sabbath work problems and be tempted not to return tithes and offerings to God. Many challenges will come our way, but we must remember that God is allowing these trials for a reason. He wants us to remain faithful to Him as we patiently wait on Him to get us through the difficult time, confidently trusting in His master plan.

Think about the disciples on the Friday of Jesus' crucifixion. All hope was gone. The One they had placed their faith in as the Messiah was dead. The future looked dark and bleak. Fear and discouragement filled their hearts. From man's perspective this was the greatest tragedy, but from God's perspective it was the greatest victory.

As Christians we will experience similar times. Events will take place that will try our faith. Yet when we know we serve a sovereign God, we can be assured that God is still with us, working out His eternal purpose in our life. We will be able to wait patiently on the Lord for deliverance.

God also allows Satan's evil plans to be carried out to a certain extent in order to vindicate God. Paul wrote of this to the Ephesians:

"His intent was that now, through the church, the manifold wisdom of God should be made known to the rulers and authorities in the heavenly realms, according to his eternal purpose which he accomplished in Christ Jesus our Lord. In him and through faith in him we may approach God with freedom and confidence. I ask you, therefore, not to be discouraged because of my suffering for you, which are your glory" (Eph. 3:10-13, NIV).

Through all of the events of earth, both good and bad from man's perspective, God will reveal His wisdom to the universe. The plans of Satan and evil men will actually work together for the vindication of God Himself. In the end "at the name of Jesus every knee shall bow, of those in heaven, and of those on earth, and of those under the earth, and . . . every tongue shall confess that Jesus Christ is Lord, to the glory of God the Father" (Phil. 2:10, 11).

It is wonderful, encouraging, and reassuring to know that God's council and plans will be carried out in our lives, in the church, and in this world. We do not serve a God who is in heaven "wishing" things would go better for His people or who is "wishing" evil men wouldn't treat His people so badly. We do not serve an impotent God. We serve a sovereign, all-powerful God whose plans are not hindered or stopped by His creation—Satan, man, or nature. The following promises reveal this truth very clearly:

"There is no wisdom, no insight, no plan that can succeed against the Lord" (Prov. 21:30, NIV).

"For the Lord of hosts has purposed, And who will annul it? His hand is stretched out, And who will turn it back?" (Isa. 14:27).

"Remember the former things of old, for I am God, and there *is* no other; I am God, and there is none like Me, declaring the end from the beginning, and from ancient times things that are not yet done, saying, 'My counsel shall stand, and I will do all My pleasure'" (Isa. 46:9, 10).

Evil men may plot and scheme against you. Satan will try to discourage and destroy you. God will allow you to go through very trying times. However, if you know beyond doubt that God is sovereign and that He will work whatever He allows to come into your life for your good, you can then wait in patient, faithful, and hopeful trust in God's divine providence. Always remember:

"Let the heavens rejoice, and let the earth be glad; and let them say among the nations, 'The Lord reigns'" (1 Chron. 16:31).

Personal Reflection and Discussion

1. Why should Christians not be surprised when difficult trials come into their lives?

_____

_____

2. How did the disciples react when Jesus was crucified? How would you have reacted?

_____

_____

3. How was the cross of Christ a good event?

_____

_____

4. What is God revealing through the events that happen to His people and church?

_____

_____

5. List two scriptures that reveal that God is sovereign over all mankind.

_____

_____

Prayer Activity

- Call your prayer partner and discuss this devotional with him/her.
- Pray with your prayer partner:
  1. for God to baptize you with His Holy Spirit.
  2. for God to revive you and His church.
  3. for God to help you remain faithful to Him in trying times.
  4. for the individuals on your prayer list.

Day 23

The Importance of Knowing God

Jesus said, "And this is eternal life, that they may know You, the only true God, and Jesus Christ, whom You have sent" (John 17:3).

Our salvation is not a matter of what we know, but whom we know. Christians who focus on only the Bible and their knowledge of Scripture are in danger of depending on "what" they know in order to be ready for Christ's second coming. As Seventh-day Adventists we feel we are secure because we know about the Sabbath, tithe paying, health reform, death, the mark of the beast, the manner of Christ's return, etc. However, remember, it was tithe-paying, Sabbathkeeping, health reformers who crucified Jesus. What we know is important, but without a personal relationship with Jesus, we will be deceived and lost in the end.

The Greek word translated "know" refers to intimate knowing, not simply an intellectual knowing. So I ask the question, Is God really real to you, or is He just an intellectual concept?

We can know things about God but not really know Him. A head knowledge of God is not real heart knowing—intimate knowing.

We don't get to know God through doctrines or teachings about Him. Israel had the Old Testament scriptures and the sanctuary service. Yet they didn't know their own God when He came in the flesh in the person of Jesus Christ. Of their lack of knowing Him, Jesus said, "You search the Scriptures, for in them you think you have eternal life; and these are they which testify of Me. But you are not willing to come to Me that you may have life" (John 5:39, 40).

We can know God is omnipotent (all powerful), omniscient (all knowing), and omnipresent (all present) without knowing Him. We can read about Creation and the other Bible stories that talk about God's power and involvement in the affairs of men and still not know Him. Such knowledge about God is not "knowing" God.

We can be very active in serving God in ministry and even do marvelous things in the name of Jesus and not know Him. Jesus pointed out this very fact in Matthew 7:21-23:

"Not everyone who says to Me, 'Lord, Lord,' shall enter the kingdom of heaven, but he who does the will of My Father in heaven. Many will say to Me in that day, 'Lord, Lord, have we not prophesied in Your name, cast out demons in Your name, and done many wonders in Your name?' And then I will declare to them, 'I never knew you; depart from Me, you who practice lawlessness!'"

Active, apparently successful ministry in the name of Jesus is not evidence of actually knowing Him. The foolish virgins were also caught up in self-deception. They believed in Jesus and that He was coming soon. They enjoyed fellowshipping with God's people. They believed the doctrines and lived the lifestyle. Yet Jesus told them, "I do not know you" (Matt. 25:12). Ellen White described them as follows:

"The class represented by the foolish virgins are not hypocrites. They have a regard for the truth, they have advocated the truth, they are attracted to those who believe the truth; but they have **not yielded themselves to the Holy Spirit's working**. . . . The class represented by the foolish virgins have been content with a superficial work. **They do not know God**. . . . Their service to God degenerates into a form" (*Christ's Object Lessons*, p. 411, emphasis added).

"The name 'foolish virgins' represents the character of those who **have not the genuine heart-work wrought by the Spirit of God**. The coming of Christ does not change the foolish virgins into wise ones. . . . The state of the church represented by the foolish virgins is also spoken of as the Laodicean state" (*Review and Herald*, Aug. 19, 1890, emphasis added).

Note that the foolish virgins do not know God because they have not yielded their lives to the working of the Holy Spirit, which would have led them to intimately knowing God and becoming like Jesus in character. This is why the daily baptism of the Holy Spirit is essential for every believer who wants to intimately know God and be ready for Christ's return.

Personal Reflection and Discussion

1. **What does the Bible mean when it says we must "know" God?**

_____

_____

2. **Is knowing truths about God the same as knowing God? How are the two different?**

_____

_____

3. **Is having an active, apparently successful ministry evidence of knowing God?**

_____

_____

4. **Why were the foolish virgins lost when Jesus, the bridegroom, returned?**

_____

_____

Prayer Activity

- **Call your prayer partner and discuss this devotional with him/her.**
- **Pray with your prayer partner:**
    1. **for God to baptize you with His Holy Spirit.**
    2. **for God to revive you and His church.**
    3. **for God to lead you into a close, knowing relationship with Him.**
    4. **for the individuals on your prayer list.**

Difficult Trials and Knowing God

There are two experiences God uses to lead us to know Him intimately and to develop a close, meaningful relationship with Him. First, He gives us the baptism of the Holy Spirit to experience every day. Second, He leads us into various life experiences. These experiences are usually what we would call difficult times in our life. Yet they are necessary for us to really come to know our God.

Old Testament Israel is a good example of God leading His people into trying situations in order for them to know Him personally. Israel had been in Egypt for 430 years. They had a head knowledge of God. They knew things about God, but they didn't really know Him intimately. First, He showed His power on their behalf against Pharaoh. They saw that God was the sovereign ruler over all nature, including death, as was demonstrated in the last plague.

As dramatic as these experiences were, Israel needed a more personal experience with their God. Therefore, God led them to the Red Sea to face a humanly impossible situation. They were trapped with Pharaoh's army behind them and the Red Sea before them.

"But lift up your rod, and stretch out your hand over the sea and divide it. And the children of Israel shall go on dry ground through the midst of the sea. And I indeed will harden the hearts of the Egyptians, and they shall follow them. So I will gain honor over Pharaoh and over all his army, his chariots, and his horsemen. . . . And Moses stretched out his hand over the sea; and when the morning appeared, the sea returned to its full depth, while the Egyptians were fleeing into it. So the Lord overthrew the Egyptians in the midst of the sea" (Ex. 14:16, 17, 27).

God brought them to a place where they had to depend 100 percent on Him for deliverance. He wanted them to learn to wait on Him in all situations and to develop complete dependence on Him. He made a way through the sea on dry land, and when Israel were safely to the other side, the sea came back together and drowned all of Pharaoh's army.

You would think that Israel would have come to know and trust God after seeing Him work personally on their behalf to deliver them from Egypt, open the Red Sea, and then destroy Pharaoh's army. Unfortunately, that was not the case. God knew they needed to be led into more difficult situations in order to get to know Him.

So, next He led them to a place where the water was undrinkable. Now this is a serious situation in the desert. They could all have died of thirst. God wanted Israel to personally, experientially come to know Him as their provider, deliverer, and savior. He wanted them to learn to wait in trusting, restful, confident faith on Him in difficult situations, knowing He would deliver.

"Now when they came to Marah, they could not drink the waters of Marah, for they were bitter. Therefore the name of it was called Marah. And the people murmured against Moses, saying, 'What shall we drink?'" So he cried out to the Lord, and the Lord showed him a tree. When he cast it into the waters, the waters were made sweet. There He made a statute and an ordinance for them, and there He tested them" (Ex. 15:23-25).

This is the purpose of all the trials of God's people—of all trials in *your* life. God leads His children into situations where they have an opportunity to learn to know and trust Him.

Personal Reflection and Discussion

1. Why did God lead Israel to the Red Sea where they could be threatened by Pharaoh's army?

_____

_____

2. Why did God lead Israel to undrinkable water in the desert where they could have died of thirst?

_____

_____

3. Why did Israel need to go through these experiences?

_____

_____

4. What experiences have you gone through in your life or are currently going through where you can see God's hand leading you to a deeper relationship with Him?

_____

_____

Prayer Activity

- Call your prayer partner and discuss this devotional with him/her.
- Pray with your prayer partner:
    1. for God to baptize you with His Holy Spirit.
    2. for God to revive you and His church.
    3. for God to help you trust Him when you are led into difficult situations.
    4. for the individuals on your prayer list.

Day 25

The Purpose of All Trials

God allows the Christian to experience trials for one purpose: that we may learn to fully trust Him with our life. We will never learn to trust Him if we never have opportunity to trust Him. Man's extremity is God's opportunity. That is why we can thank God for all things and that all things, even difficult situations, will work together for our good and God's glory.

"In everything give thanks; for this is the will of God in Christ Jesus for you" (1 Thess. 5:18).

"And we know that all things work together for good to those who love God, to those who are the called according to His purpose" (Rom. 8:28).

In every trial we go through, God wants us to learn something about Him. We see this in the story of Jesus' friend Lazarus' sickness and death. Lazarus' sisters, Martha and Mary, sent for Jesus to come heal their brother. Jesus delayed His coming to them. Martha and Mary could have concluded that Jesus didn't care about the crisis they were in with their brother facing death. Yet, Jesus had a purpose in His delay. He wanted to reveal something to them about Himself—that He is not only the great healer of disease and sickness but also the resurrection and the life:

"Jesus said to her, 'I am the resurrection and the life. He who believes in Me, though he may die, he shall live'" (John 11:25).

He also wanted Martha and Mary to learn the lesson of waiting on God in restful faith, assured that He will do all things well. This is the same lesson He wants us to learn in every trial. The sooner we learn this lesson the sooner we will experience the peace that passes all understanding in every trial of life—many times He seems not to hear or answer our prayers, because we have not learned to trust Him. Trusting God comes only as we intimately know Him.

God often uses financial and material needs to lead us into a closer relationship with Him. We may think we know God and trust Him, but when we face a major financial crisis, we discover our faith is not as strong as we thought.

For example, in Malachi God promises to bless us if we return tithes and offerings to Him. This is the only Bible verse where God asks us to "prove" Him or put Him to the "test" on the matter. God knows that money is an area where our faith can waver if we don't think we have enough to give a tithe to God. So God leads us to a situation where we have an opportunity to put Him to the test, to prove Him faithful. At such times He wants us to lean on His promises such as:

"Seek first the kingdom of God and His righteousness, and all these things shall be added to you" (Matt. 6:33).

"Honor the Lord with your possessions, and with the firstfruits of all your increase; so your barns will be filled with plenty, and your vats will overflow with new wine" (Prov. 3:9, 10).

Notice, we are told to honor God first. Then we can claim in faith His promise to provide. This is exactly what Jesus said: "seek first the kingdom of God . . . and" all we need will be added to us. I can say from experience that many times God will not bring deliverance until we step out in faith to follow His counsel and commands. He will allow us to enter into trying situations for us to learn the important lesson of trusting in Him for deliverance.

Do you really believe what God says? Do you

know God personally enough to really trust Him in all situations, even the most difficult and trying ones? This is the very purpose He has in allowing us to go through difficult times. He wants us to learn that we can wait on Him in trusting, restful faith, knowing without doubt that He will deliver us in His own way and time. Those ready to meet Jesus when He comes will be a people who know by experience that they can confidently trust their God, knowing that He will deliver them even when everything seems to be against them and their enemies are saying their God has deserted them.

Personal Reflection and Discussion

1. Why did Jesus delay in responding to Martha and Mary's request concerning their brother Lazarus?

_____

_____

2. Why does God lead His children into difficult situations?

_____

_____

3. What kind of difficult situations does God often use to teach His children to trust Him?

_____

_____

4. What should be the Christian's attitude in all situations? What is your attitude in all situations?

_____

_____

5. When you face a difficult financial situation what should you do in relation to returning tithes and offerings to God?

_____

_____

6. Read Numbers 23:19. Does God ever lie? Does this text give you assurance and strengthen your faith?

_____

_____

Prayer Activity

- Call your prayer partner and discuss this devotional with him/her.
- Pray with your prayer partner:
    1. for God to baptize you with His Holy Spirit.
    2. for God to revive you and His church.
    3. for God to help you trust Him in all situations.
    4. for God to continue helping you through life's trials, thanking Him for His guidance in the past.
    5. for the individuals on your prayer list.

Day 26

Why Brokenness Is Necessary

Today's devotional presents one of the most important teachings that Christians need to understand in order to be able to wait on God in faithful, hopeful trust during the darkest hours of their walk with the Lord. It is something that all Christians must experience to some degree. What is this experience? It is brokenness: the process of God breaking our pride and selfish spirit.

The Bible warns us of the dangers of pride.

"Pride *goes* before destruction, and a haughty spirit before a fall" (Prov. 16:18).

It is a very dangerous thing for God to use a man or woman in a very powerful way. It could destroy them spiritually. Sinful human nature is prone to allow pride and self-exaltation to take over, which could lead to serious sins. We have seen examples of well-known Christian celebrities who received human accolades and praise. In due time they fell into sin because of pride, self-confidence, power, and wealth.

The greater the brokenness in one's life, the greater our usefulness to God:

"The sacrifices of God are a broken spirit, a broken and contrite heart—these, O God, You will not despise" (Ps. 51:17).

"Therefore humble yourselves under the mighty hand of God, that He may exalt you in due time" (1 Peter 5:6).

The way to true greatness in God's work is first humbleness through breaking and then exaltation. The truly humble will never seek the highest position, set personal goals of self-advancement, or seek recognition for their achievements. They are content to serve God in whatever capacity He calls them, whether considered a high or lowly position by man.

God wants all of His servants to strive to obtain this attitude of humility. Therefore, He leads them into varied situations to bring this about in their lives:

"'For whom the Lord loves He chastens, and scourges every son whom He receives.' If you endure chastening, God deals with you as with sons; for what son is there whom a father does not chasten? . . . Now no chastening seems to be joyful for the present, but grievous; nevertheless, afterward it yields the peaceable fruit of righteousness to those who have been trained by it" (Heb. 12:6, 7, 11).

The breaking experience is from God. It is God's discipline and is never pleasant. Breaking times are the dark times in one's experience. They are times when our prayers seem not to be heard and God seems far away and uncaring. They are often times when we feel unproductive in God's service. Broken experiences are often times of severe temptation and even a major fall. Yet, in the end it will produce glorious results in God's children. Of this Paul wrote: "We must through many tribulations enter the kingdom of God" (Acts 14:22). Trials are the means God uses to develop in us endurance, faith, and humility—Christ's character.

Pride is a symptom of not being broken. Pride is deceitful. We can think we are humble and not self-seeking, and yet pride is very much a part of our life. The Bible tells us that the "heart is deceitful above all things, and desperately wicked; who can know it?" (Jer. 17:9).

It is important for us to become aware of the evidences of whether we are proud or broken. Humble people do not consider themselves great; they are small in their own eyes. They always give God or others the credit for any success they experience. The humble will not let a perceived weakness or inability keep them from serving God.

Pride gets in the way of God being able to use us most effectively. It also gets in the way of our happiness. Ellen White wrote:

"It is the love of self that destroys our peace. While self is all alive, we stand ready continually to guard it from mortification and insult; but when we are dead and our life is hid with Christ in God, we shall not take neglects or slights to heart. We shall be deaf to reproach and blind to scorn and insult" (*Thoughts From the Mount of Blessing*, p. 16).

What amazing statements. When we are broken and pride is subdued, we will not take it to heart when someone scorns or insults us. We will be able to immediately let it go. Why? Because if we are humble through brokenness, we are not constantly seeking to exalt self and protect it from insult.

Personal Reflection and Discussion

1. What is a major barrier to God using us in a significant way?

_____

_____

2. How does God break our pride?

_____

_____

3. What are the characteristics of the breaking experience?

_____

_____

4. If I get my feelings hurt easily what does that say about me?

_____

_____

5. What are the characteristics of humility?

_____

_____

Prayer Activity

- **Call your prayer partner and discuss this devotional with him/her.**
- **Pray with your prayer partner:**
    1. **for God to baptize you with His Holy Spirit.**
    2. **for God to revive you and His church.**
    3. **for God to lead you to overcome all pride in your life.**
    4. **for the individuals on your prayer list.**

Pride is the opposite of humility. Where there is humility, there will be love. Paul described the opposite of pride when he listed the characteristics of genuine Christian love: "Love is very patient and kind, never jealous or envious, never boastful or proud, never haughty or selfish or rude. Love does not demand its own way. It is not irritable or touchy. It does not hold grudges and will hardly even notice when others do it wrong. It is never glad about injustice, but rejoices whenever truth wins out. If you love someone you will be loyal to him no matter what the cost. You will always believe in him, always expect the best of him, and always stand your ground in defending him" (1 Cor. 13:4-7, TLB).

There are many examples in the Bible of God leading His children into experiences that break their pride, fear, and self-sufficiency. Abraham, the father of the faithful, did not begin as such. He was fearful, having great concern for self. He lied two times about his wife being his sister in order to protect himself. God brought Abraham into situations designed to break his pride and selfishness. The final and greatest test was to offer his only son, whom he loved very much, to God as a sacrifice. Abraham finally came to the place of breaking, and God could make him a great blessing to others.

"Then the Angel of the Lord called to Abraham a second time out of heaven, and said: 'By Myself I have sworn, says the Lord, because you have done this thing, and have not withheld your son, your only son, in blessing I will bless you, and multiplying I will multiply your descendants as the stars of the heaven and as the sand which is on the seashore; and your descendants shall possess the gate of their enemies. In your seed all the nations of the earth shall be blessed, because you have obeyed My voice'" (Gen. 22:15-18).

This breaking process was not a pleasant experience for Abraham. Breaking trials never are. Yet, they are necessary for all Christians to go through.

Moses is a clear example of a proud man being broken by God in order to do a great work for Him. When he was a young man, Moses was ready to deliver Israel. By killing the Egyptian, he thought that Israel would rally around his leadership and fight against their masters. This didn't happen. So in fear for his life, he fled Egypt. His initial breaking took 40 years of shepherding sheep in the desert. Then when God called him to return to Egypt to deliver Israel, Moses felt very incapable, and he said to God: "Who am I that I should go to Pharaoh, and that I should bring the children of Israel out of Egypt?" (Ex. 3:11).

He was broken and humbled by the experience of the past 40 years. Now he was ready to be used mightily by God to deliver Israel. Moses' breaking also continued during the next 40 years of desert wandering.

We see the same process time and again in the lives of God's children throughout the Bible. Christ's disciples were proud men, even arguing about who was to have the highest position in His kingdom as they made their way to the first Communion service. When Jesus was taken, they all fled in fear. They were broken, discouraged men. This brokenness was necessary for them to become mighty preachers of the gospel and the founding apostles of the Christian church.

Every Christian must experience brokenness. We are naturally proud and self-focused. We naturally like and seek applause and high positions. All this must change in order for God to use us in any significant way.

Personal Reflection and Discussion

1. Pride is the opposite of _____.

2. Humility in the Christian's life has the same characteristics as _____.

3. List the characteristics of love Paul gives in 1 Corinthians 13.

_____

_____

_____

4. Why is brokenness necessary in the Christian's life?

_____

_____

5. Have you experienced brokenness in Christ?

_____

_____

Prayer Activity

- Call your prayer partner and discuss this devotional with him/her.
- Pray with your prayer partner:
    1. for God to baptize you with His Holy Spirit.
    2. for God to revive you and His church.
    3. for God to break you and rid your life of any pride that would keep you from Him.
    4. for the individuals on your prayer list.

Breaking Through Trials and Difficulties

Brokenness, trials, and difficult times are very painful to experience. They are dark times when we don't understand what God is doing. They can be times of sorrow, confusion, and even despair. They are times when our patience and our ability to trust and wait on God are challenged. However, they are times when we will learn that we *can* wait on God in this manner, knowing He will see us through the difficulty and bring it to a glorious end:

"Behold, the eye of the Lord is on those who fear Him, on those who hope in His mercy, to deliver their soul from death, and to keep them alive in famine. Our soul waits for the Lord; He is our help and our shield. For our heart shall rejoice in Him, because we have trusted in His holy name. Let Your mercy, O Lord, be upon us, just as we hope in You" (Ps. 33:18-22).

These breaking times will transform us as Peter and the other disciples were. The breaking process breaks our proud hearts, removes the desire for self-exaltation, humbles our inflated egos, and leads us to one goal in life: to faithfully serve God.

As a result we will experience a depth of relationship with God as never before. We will see God minister through us as never before. We will see the power of God as never before, and we will see Christ and Christ alone exalted in our life.

It is important to understand the breaking process. If we do not understand it, we may become discouraged and bitter, believing that God doesn't care and doesn't love us.

Also, we must realize that brokenness is a continuing process. There may be one major breaking time in our life, but the breaking process continues through-

out life. Paul experienced an initial breaking at his conversion:

"Then Saul, still breathing threats and murder against the disciples of the Lord, went to the high priest and asked letters from him to the synagogues of Damascus, so that if he found any who were of the Way, whether men or women, he might bring them bound to Jerusalem. As he journeyed he came near Damascus, and suddenly a light shone around him from heaven. Then he fell to the ground, and heard a voice saying to him, 'Saul, Saul, why are you persecuting Me?' And he said, 'Who are You, Lord?' " (Acts 9:1-5).

That was Saul's initial breaking experience. But God continued to allow him to experience ongoing trials and difficulties in order to keep him humble:

"And lest I should be exalted above measure by the abundance of the revelations, a thorn in the flesh was given to me, a messenger of Satan to buffet me, lest I be exalted above measure. Concerning this thing I pleaded with the Lord three times that it might depart from me. And He said to me, 'My grace is sufficient for you, for My strength is made perfect in weakness.' Therefore most gladly I will rather boast in my infirmities, that the power of Christ may rest upon me. Therefore I take pleasure in infirmities, in reproaches, in needs, in persecutions, in distresses, for Christ's sake. For when I am weak, then I am strong" (2 Cor. 12:7-10).

Many years ago, the pastor who baptized me shared a statement that his daughter had written in the flyleaf of one of her books. It read something like this, "The test of true Christianity is when we can thank God for someone else's success where we have failed." This is also evidence of brokenness.

When we understand that brokenness is the goal of the trials we go through, then we are better able to wait on God in trusting, hopeful faith, knowing that He will be with us in the trial and will fulfill His promise to work it out for our good and His glory.

God reminds everyone who is going through diffi-cult times to "Wait on the Lord; be of good courage, and He shall strengthen your heart; wait, I say, on the Lord" (Ps. 27:14). "For the Lord will not cast off for-ever. Though He causes grief, yet He will show com-passion according to the multitude of His mercies" (Lam. 3:31, 32).

"Wait on the Lord; be of good courage, and He shall strengthen your heart; wait I say on the Lord"

(Psalm 27:14).

Personal Reflection and Discussion

1. Describe what it is like for the Christian to go through breaking experiences.

_____

_____

2. What is God's goal for you when He takes you through breaking experiences?

_____

_____

3. If Christians do not understand the breaking process, what can happen to their relationship with God?

_____

_____

4. Is the breaking process a one-time experience or is it continuous?

_____

_____

Prayer Activity

● Call your prayer partner and discuss this devotional with him/her.
● Pray with your prayer partner:
    1. for God to baptize you with His Holy Spirit.
    2. for God to revive you and His church.
    3. for God to help you understand and accept what is happening when you go through breaking times in your life.
    4. for the individuals on your prayer list.

Day 29
Our Fourth Watch God: Part 1

In Matthew 14 we read about Jesus feeding the 5,000. It had been a wonderful day of preaching the gospel and performing the miracle of feeding more than 5,000 people using just five loaves of bread and two fish. Afterward, He sent the multitude away, and He directed the disciples to go to the other side of the lake. Then Jesus went up into the mountain to pray.

The disciples were making their way across the lake when a storm arose, and the wind and waves tossed the boat around, threatening the lives of the disciples. As they were struggling to keep the boat afloat, they saw the figure of a man walking on the water. They became fearful and cried out, thinking it was a ghost:

"But the boat was now in the middle of the sea, tossed by the waves, for the wind was contrary. Now in the fourth watch of the night Jesus went to them, walking on the sea. And when the disciples saw Him walking on the sea, they were troubled, saying, 'It is a ghost!' And they cried out for fear. But immediately Jesus spoke to them, saying, 'Be of good cheer! It is I; do not be afraid'" (Matt. 14:24-27).

The disciples were in danger of their boat sinking in the storm; they could have lost their lives. They struggled through the night. But in the fourth watch Jesus appeared to deliver them, and He said, "Be of good cheer! It is I; do not be afraid."

The disciples were in the stormy situation by following Jesus' directions. They hadn't presumptuously placed themselves in danger. This is an important lesson to us. We don't want to presumptuously put ourselves in harm's way either, but sometimes we end up in a dangerous situation because we are following God's will.

Although we may face challenging situations, we can be assured we are directed by God when we seek the baptism of the Holy Spirit every day, ask God for guidance in everything, ask God for wisdom to make good decisions, and trust that the Lord will answer our prayers. God promises: "I will instruct you and teach you in the way you should go; I will guide you with My eye" (Ps. 32:8). We must learn to wait on the Lord for His direction in all things and all decisions.

One lesson we learn from this story of the disciples is that following Jesus is not always the easiest path. Following Jesus' directions does not mean we will avoid problems in life. Yet, we can be assured that in every problem God allows to come our way there is a purpose. The purpose God has for us when He allows us to experience problems and difficulties is for us to get to know Him better as a loving, caring heavenly Father.

Another lesson we can learn from this story is by observing when Jesus came to deliver the disciples from the storm. It was during the fourth watch (Matt. 14:25). In the Hebrew culture there were four watches in the night: first watch, 6:00 to 9:00 p.m.; second watch, 9:00 p.m. to midnight; third watch, midnight to 3:00 a.m., and fourth watch, 3:00 to 6:00 a.m. The fourth watch was the last watch before dawn, which is the darkest time. Many times God comes to deliver us during the fourth watch, at the darkest time when all seems hopeless and lost. Our God is often a fourth watch God.

God does this because He wants us to learn to wait patiently and confidently on Him. Instead of worrying about the situation, in trusting peace we can rest on His promise to deliver and provide for us.

We see God acting in the "fourth watch" in the lives of many Bible characters. Throughout the Bible we read of situations God allowed to happen that required waiting patiently on God, even in the face of the most trying circumstances. We see this in the history of Abraham, Hagar, Ishmael, and Isaac. God waited until Abraham and his wife were beyond childbearing years to fulfill His promise of a son. God waited until the last second to stay Abraham's hand when he was about to thrust the knife into Isaac's chest. And God waited until Hagar had lost all hope of her and her son surviving in the desert to reveal water.

When we learn the lesson of waiting on God in patient, restful faith during our most trying times, we will have a peace that "passes understanding" and will bring glory to God (Phil. 4:6, 7). God wants us to learn not to worry or become anxious over any situation we find ourselves in. God has promised to deliver us. However, He often waits until the fourth watch to bring about our deliverance.

Personal Reflection and Discussion

1. Why did the disciples find themselves in a boat in the storm?
_____
_____

2. When did Jesus appear to deliver them from the storm?
_____
_____

3. What spiritual lesson do we learn from the story of Jesus delivering the disciples during the fourth watch?
_____
_____

4. List other Bible characters who were delivered during the "fourth watch"?
_____
_____

5. Why does God often wait until the "fourth watch" of our crisis to deliver us?
_____
_____

Prayer Activity

- Call your prayer partner and discuss this devotional with him/her.
- Pray with your prayer partner:
    1. for God to baptize you with His Holy Spirit.
    2. for God to revive you and His church.
    3. for God to lead you to trust Him, even into the fourth watch of any crisis in your life.
    4. for the individuals on your prayer list.

There are times when God delivers us during the first watch. When we ask for forgiveness, he immediately forgives us:

"If we confess our sins, He is faithful and just to forgive us our sins, and to cleanse us from all unrighteousness" (1 John 1:9).

I have also found that He provides emotional deliverance quickly, since this facet is important to developing the intimate relationship He wants us to have with Him. God's Spirit desires to fill our hearts with love, joy, peace, and faith. He doesn't want us to be oppressed with overwhelming negative emotions.

As we saw in yesterday's devotional, many times God delivers us in the fourth watch, when things seem most hopeless and lost. At such times it is essential we remember God will always deliver and meet our needs: spiritually, emotionally, physically, and materially. David knew this truth when he wrote:

"The angel of the Lord encamps all around those who fear Him, and delivers them. Oh, taste and see that the Lord is good; blessed is the man who trusts in Him! Oh, fear the Lord, you His saints! There is no want to those who fear Him. . . . The eyes of the Lord are on the righteous, and His ears are open to their cry. . . . The righteous cry out, and the Lord hears, and delivers them out of all their troubles. The Lord is near to those who have a broken heart, and saves such as have a contrite spirit. Many are the afflictions of the righteous, but the Lord delivers him out of them all. . . . The Lord redeems the soul of His servants, and none of those who trust in Him shall be condemned" (Ps. 34:7-22).

The key to deliverance is stated in the following verses also:

"But without faith it is impossible to please Him, for he who comes to God must believe that He is, and that He is a rewarder of those who diligently seek Him" (Heb. 11:6).

"The Lord is good to those who wait for Him, to the soul who seeks Him. It is good that one should hope and wait quietly for the salvation of the Lord" (Lam. 3:25, 26).

Christians will have trials and difficulties. Our faith will be tested. But the purpose of the trials is to give us an opportunity to get to know our loving, compassionate heavenly Father better. We must never stop waiting in prayer—trusting and believing that God will hear and deliver us in His own time and way. Often His deliverance will come in the fourth watch when all seems hopeless and lost.

Scripture indicates that there is a direct relationship between our waiting on God in hopeful faith and the blessings we receive:

"Behold, the eye of the Lord is on those who fear Him, on those who hope in His mercy, to deliver their soul from death, and to keep them alive in famine. Our soul waits for the Lord; He is our help and our shield. For our heart shall rejoice in Him, because we have trusted in His holy name. Let Your mercy, O Lord, be upon us, **just as we hope** in You" (Ps. 33:18-22, emphasis added).

Notice that the scripture says that God's mercy will be upon us "just as we hope" in Him. The more we trust and hopefully wait on God the more we will see God's power in our life.

Those ready to meet Jesus will experience fourth watch deliverance. It is when all earthly sup-

port has been withdrawn, when the decree has been passed to put them to death that Christ will deliver us. It is essential that we—the last generation of Christians—learn the lesson of patiently waiting on God in faithful, restful trust even when God delays His deliverance. If we don't learn this lesson, we will be in danger of giving up our faith when the tough times come. You may be going through such a time of waiting right now. If so, this is the lesson the Lord is seeking to teach you. Stay faithful during this time of "darkness and confusion" and learn the lesson of waiting on God. He may wait until the fourth watch to deliver you, but be assured, He will deliver you.

Personal Reflection and Discussion

1. Does God always wait until the fourth watch to deliver us? Give an example of God delivering as soon as we ask.

_____

_____

2. Why does God often wait until the fourth watch to deliver us?

_____

_____

3. Why must Christians who are living when Jesus returns learn to wait patently in faith for God's deliverance? If they haven't learned to wait on God's deliverance what do you think will happen to them?

_____

_____

Prayer Activity

- Call your prayer partner and discuss this devotional with him/her.
- Pray with your prayer partner:
    1. for God to baptize you with His Holy Spirit.
    2. for God to revive you and His church.
    3. for God to teach you to trust Him no matter what He allows to come into your life.
    4. for the individuals on your prayer list.

Day 31

The Storms of Life

When we pray for God's will to be done in our life, we will often be caught in a stormy situation. It is easy for us to become fearful and anxious at such times. The storms of life try our faith, revealing our faith or lack of faith. The storms also give us an opportunity to develop faith—to develop Christ's character.

God uses storms, trying and difficult experiences, to carry out His will in our life. When we learn to trust in God, all fear, anxiety, and concern will be gone, and peace will fill our heart. We find many biblical examples of God's people being caught in a storm.

The story of Joseph, the son of Jacob, is one such story. Jacob loved Joseph very much, and he gave him a coat of many colors. After receiving the coat, Joseph had dreams that seemed to indicate that his family would bow down to him sometime in the future.

Jacob's special treatment of Joseph had created flaws in his son's character. In order for God to be able to carry out His plans in Joseph's life, it was necessary for Joseph to go through several storms to develop the character God needed so that He could use him in a mighty way. Ellen White wrote of Joseph's experience:

"But, in the providence of God, even this experience was to be a blessing to him. He had learned in a few hours that which years might not otherwise have taught him. His father, strong and tender as his love had been, had done him wrong by his partiality and indulgence. This unwise preference had angered his brothers and provoked them to the cruel deed that had separated him from his home. Its effects were manifest also in his own character. Faults had been encouraged that were now to be corrected. He was becoming self-sufficient and exacting. Accustomed to the tenderness of his father's care, he felt that he was unprepared to cope with the difficulties before him, in the bitter, uncared-for life of a stranger and a slave" (*Patriarchs and Prophets*, p. 213).

Joseph proved to be faithful to God and man when he was brought to Egypt. However, the storms continued. As you know from an earlier devotional, Joseph was tempted, tested, and thrown into prison. Through all of these situations, Joseph had to rely on God and continue praying for God's will be done in his life. However, as God's will was performed in Joseph's life, he was caught in the storm. It was through adversity that God fulfilled the dreams he gave to Joseph. If there had been no slave sale and imprisonment, there would have been no governorship in Egypt, and there would have been no saving of Jacob's family from the famine. Ellen White wrote:

"Trials and obstacles are the Lord's chosen methods of discipline and His appointed conditions of success" (*The Ministry of Healing*, p. 471).

Throughout the story of Joseph we see him patiently waiting on and looking to God for deliverance. Many things happened to him that he didn't understand. I am sure that at times it seemed as if God had forsaken him. Yet, he still trusted God to see him through the storms and deliver him. By trusting and waiting on God, Joseph received a great blessing as he endured the severe storms of life that the Lord allowed him to experience.

Joseph's story is a lesson for us. When thrown into a severe storm of life, God wants us to know that we are in the storm by His providence and that He has a divine purpose for our life. Even if we find ourselves in a storm by our own foolish actions, God will use that to teach us important life lessons, and we will learn how truly merciful and forgiving He is. The psalmist tells us:

"Fools, because of their transgression, and because of their iniquities, were afflicted. Their soul abhorred all manner of food, and they drew near to the gates of death. Then they cried out to the Lord in their trouble, and He saved them out of their distresses. He sent His word and healed them, and delivered them from their destructions" (Ps. 107:17-20).

Our God is sovereign and capable to deliver us from our own foolishness. We may suffer from it, but even these storms will work out for our good and God's glory.

Personal Reflection and Discussion

1. Why does God allow storms to come into the Christian's life?

_____

_____

2. What lessons did God teach Joseph through the storms He led him to experience?

_____

_____

3. List a few stormy experiences God has allowed to come into your life and the lessons you have learned.

_____

_____

4. Can the Christian learn lessons from storms brought on by their own foolishness?

_____

_____

Prayer Activity

- Call your prayer partner and discuss this devotional with him/her.
- Pray with your prayer partner:
    1. for God to baptize you with His Holy Spirit.
    2. for God to revive you and His church.
    3. for God to lead you to trust Him even through the worst of life's storms.
    4. for God to keep you from foolishly bringing a needless storm into your life.
    5. for the individuals on your prayer list.

Why the Storms of Life Are Necessary

God will let the storms rage in our life. Like the refiner's fire, He will use these storms to develop Christ's character in areas where we need changing. This process will especially intensify as we approach Christ's return. Those ready to meet Jesus will have gone through the refining process, enabling Christ to be perfectly reflected in their character. Trials and difficulties are the means God uses to carry on His work of purification in our life:

"Christ is waiting with longing desire for the manifestation of Himself in His church. When the character of Christ shall be perfectly reproduced in His people, then He will come to claim them as His own" (*Christ's Object Lessons*, p. 69).

The storms of life can be confusing and scary, but we must remember who is with us. Take for example the story of the disciples and their experience on the stormy seas:

"On the same day, when evening had come, He said to them, 'Let us cross over to the other side.' Now when they had left the multitude, they took Him along in the boat as He was. And other little boats were also with Him. And a great windstorm arose, and the waves beat into the boat, so that it was already filling. But He was in the stern, asleep on a pillow. And they awoke Him and said to Him, 'Teacher, do You not care that we are perishing?' Then He arose and rebuked the wind, and said to the sea, 'Peace, be still!' And the wind ceased and there was a great calm. But He said to them, 'Why are you so fearful? How is it that you have no faith?'" (Mark 4:35-40).

The disciples and Jesus were caught in a terrible storm in a small boat on the lake. The disciples fought the storm, trying to keep the boat afloat, but they couldn't do it on their own. Jesus was asleep in the back of the boat. They cried out to Him in desperation, "Teacher, do You not care that we are perishing?" Jesus words of reply are very significant, "Why are you so fearful? How is it that you have no faith?"

The point of the story is not that Jesus can stop the storm, even though that is good to know. The point is, don't fight the storm. The disciples were in the storm at Jesus' direction, and Jesus was with the disciples in the boat.

Ellen White wrote of the great peace Jesus had when He ministered on earth. Describing His response during the storm, she wrote:

"When Jesus was awakened to meet the storm, he was in perfect peace. There was no trace of fear in word or look, for no fear was in His heart. But He rested not in the possession of almighty power. It was not as the 'Master of earth and sea and sky' that He reposed in quiet. That power He had laid down, and He says, 'I can of Mine own self do nothing.' John 5:30. He trusted in the Father's might. It was in faith—faith in God's love and care—that Jesus rested, and the power of that word which stilled the storm was the power of God" (*The Desire of Ages*, p. 336).

She goes on to challenge us to trust our Lord in the same manner:

"As Jesus rested by faith in the Father's care, so we are to rest in the care of our Saviour. If the disciples had trusted in Him, they would have been kept in peace. Their fear in the time of danger revealed their unbelief. In their efforts to save themselves, they forgot Jesus: and it was only when, in despair of self-dependence,

they turned to Him that He could give them help.

"How often the disciples' experience is ours! When the tempests of temptation gather, and the fierce lightnings flash, and the waves sweep over us, we battle with the storm alone, forgetting that there is One who can help us. We trust in our own strength till our hope is lost, and we are ready to perish. Then we remember Jesus, and if we call upon Him to save us, we shall not cry in vain. . . . Whether on the land or on the sea, if we have the Saviour in our hearts, there is no need of fear. Living faith in the Redeemer will smooth the sea of life, and will deliver us from danger in the way that He knows to be best" (*ibid*.).

The same lesson applies to us today. The storms of life are inevitable; we will experience trying and difficult times. However, we do not have to fight the storm. Jesus is with us in the boat of life, and He will not leave you during the storms of life.

WHY THE STORMS OF LIFE ARE NECESSARY / DAY 32

Personal Reflection and Discussion

1. Why does God allow storms to rage in our lives?

_____

_____

2. What is Christ waiting for in His people? What must happen before His return?

_____

_____

3. What lessons can be learned from the disciples' stormy experience on the lake?

_____

_____

_____

_____

Prayer Activity

- Call your prayer partner and discuss this devotional with him/her.
- Pray with your prayer partner:
    1. for God to baptize you with His Holy Spirit.
    2. for God to revive you and His church.
    3. for God to lead you to trust Him.
    4. for God to help you not to panic when storms come into your life.
    5. for the individuals on your prayer list.

Day 33

Fear Not

There is no need for Christians to fear anything. Satan was defeated at the cross of Christ, and Christ's victory is ours.

Fear is the opposite of faith. Therefore, fearfulness is the same as faithlessness. God warns us of the serious consequences of being fearful in the last days:

"He who overcomes shall inherit all things, and I will be his God and he shall be My son. But the cowardly, unbelieving, abominable, murderers, sexually immoral, sorcerers, idolaters, and all liars shall have their part in the lake which burns with fire and brimstone, which is the second death" (Rev. 21:7, 8).

Jesus indicated that little real faith will exist on earth when He returns: "Nevertheless, when the Son of Man comes, will He really find faith on the earth?" (Luke 18:8). This will be true even among many professed Christians. In the last days most Christians will have "a form of godliness, but denying its power" (2 Tim. 3:5). It is essential that those living when Jesus comes are men and women of faith who have learned the lessons of waiting on God in trusting, hopeful faith. They have learned that they need not fear anything because they serve a sovereign God who rules in heaven and earth.

How many times have you heard Christians say, I'm worried about my job, my finances, my future, what's going to happen to me, my retirement, my children, the next hurricane, my health. . . . Only those with a strong faith will be ready for Christ's return.

In order to strengthen our faith, Jesus allows us to go through difficult situations now. We must learn to trust Him and His Word. Faith does not believe God *can do* what He says. Faith believes God *will do* what He says. In fact, fear is faith in the devil, believing he will do what he says he will do and God can't stop him. Fear gives Satan right of passage in our life in the areas we fear.

Job made a significant statement when he said, "For the thing I greatly feared has come upon me, and what I dreaded has happened to me" (Job 3:25).

This text clearly reveals that Satan has the right to attack us in the areas we fear. Why? Because we are putting our trust in Satan rather than in God in those areas of our life. Faith, on the other hand, gives God right of passage into our life in the areas we are placing our faith in Him.

We need not fear because Jesus has all power in heaven and earth: "Then Jesus came and spoke to them, saying, 'All authority has been given to Me in heaven and on earth'" (Matt. 28:18).

All things are under His authority: "the eyes of your understanding being enlightened; that you may know what is the hope of His calling, what are the riches of the glory of His inheritance in the saints, and what is the exceeding greatness of His power toward us who believe, according to the working of His mighty power which He worked in Christ when He raised Him from the dead and seated Him at His right hand in the heavenly places, far above all principality and power and might and dominion, and every name that is named, not only in this age but also in that which is to come. And He put all things under His feet, and gave Him *to be* head over all things to the church" (Eph. 1:18-22).

As believers in Jesus Christ we have all authority and power in His name: "Behold, I give you the authority to trample on serpents and scorpions, and over all the power of the enemy, and nothing shall by any means hurt you" (Luke 10:19).

Knowing these truths about our position with Christ we should not fear anything: man, nature, sickness or disease, financial crisis, or Satan in any form. "Yet in all these things we are more than conquerors through Him who loved us" (Rom. 8:37). We have God's promises and we have Christ who is exalted in sovereign authority above all things in heaven and earth—over Satan, man, and nature. Jesus is sovereign over all situations and circumstances. Therefore, the believer in Jesus Christ should never be fearful. Instead of fear, we must learn to wait in trusting, hopeful faith for God's deliverance no matter what we are facing. That is the attitude all must have who will be ready to meet Jesus when He comes.

Personal Reflection and Discussion

1. How serious of a matter is fear in the Christian's life?

_____

_____

2. What is fear's relationship to faith?

_____

_____

3. When we fear, who are we putting our faith in? Do you struggle with fear?

_____

_____

4. When we fear, what right of passage does our fear give Satan?

_____

_____

5. Why should the Christian not fear anything?

_____

_____

Prayer Activity

● **Call your prayer partner and discuss this devotional with him/her.**

● **Pray with your prayer partner:**

    1. for God to baptize you with His Holy Spirit.

    2. for God to revive you and His church.

    3. for God to forgive you for fearing and doubting His promises.

    4. for God to give you the faith to believe what He says.

    5. for the individuals on your prayer list.

Day 34

Righteousness by Faith Alone

The great controversy has always been over Christ. We read in the book of Revelation about when the controversy first began in heaven: "And war broke out in heaven: Michael and his angels fought against the dragon; and the dragon and his angels fought" (Rev. 12:7).

Satan hates Christ and has always tried to replace Him: "I will ascend above the heights of the clouds, I will be like the Most High" (Isa. 14:14).

The same controversy takes place in the lives of men and women today. Satan desires to reign on the throne of the heart. He wants people to follow his ways, not Christ's ways. In the area of Christian living, he wants to replace Christ's righteousness with man's efforts. He wants them to look to their own efforts for righteousness rather than Christ and His righteousness. He wants them to look to themselves for obedience rather than to Christ manifesting His obedience in and through them.

This issue was at the heart of the Protestant Reformation. The battle cry of the reformation was *sola fide*, "by faith alone." This issue is at the heart of the gospel and the message of righteousness by faith.

The Bible is clear on the matter. Concerning the Christian's walk with God, Paul wrote: "As you have therefore received Christ Jesus the Lord, so walk in Him" (Col. 2:6).

The way one receives Jesus Christ as Savior is by faith. We must believe that Jesus is the Son of God, that He died for our sins, that He forgives our sins, and that He gives us eternal life. One becomes a Christian by faith in Christ. Works are not involved.

God does not require a lost sinner to begin doing good works before coming to Christ. The sinner does not have to "clean up" his life and try to make himself acceptable to God before receiving salvation. No, the sinner simply comes to Christ as he is, accepting Jesus by faith as His Savior.

Once we are born again and begin seeking to live the Christian life it is natural for us to focus on our own efforts to obey God's law. However, we soon discover that this is impossible. Paul described this impossibility:

"I find then a law, that evil is present with me, the one who wills to do good. For I delight in the law of God according to the inward man. But I see another law in my members, warring against the law of my mind, and bringing me into captivity to the law of sin which is in my members" (Rom. 7:21-23).

Paul had personally experienced the impossibility of obeying God's law through his own efforts. He was forced to cry out, "O wretched man that I am! Who will deliver me from this body of death?" (verse 24).

He then gives the answer to his cry: "I thank God— through Jesus Christ our Lord!" (verse 25).

The apostle Paul had learned that faith in Christ was the only way to victoriously live the Christian life. Of this he wrote: "For what the law could not do in that it was weak through the flesh, God did by sending His own Son in the likeness of sinful flesh, on account of sin: He condemned sin in the flesh, that the righteous requirement of the law might be fulfilled in us who do not walk according to the flesh but according to the Spirit" (Rom. 8:3, 4).

In order to walk in the Spirit, one must daily experience the baptism of the Holy Spirit and choose to yield to the Spirit's promptings. Once the choice is

made to yield to the Spirit's promptings, we are then to look to Christ to live out His victory over the temptation in our life.

Jesus "was in all points tempted as we are, yet without sin" (Heb. 4:15). Because of Jesus' perfect, righteous obedience to God's law, when we have Jesus living in us we have His righteous obedience available to us. Therefore, Paul stated that "the righteous requirement of the law might be fulfilled in us" (Rom. 8:4).

You see, because of the "weakness" of our flesh, we are unable to fulfill the righteous requirements of the law. However, if we have Jesus living in us through the baptism of the Holy Spirit, He will live out His righteous obedience "in us" if we place our "faith" in Him to do so. This is how we have Christ's righteousness manifested in our life by faith. We can be righteous only by faith in Christ and His righteous obedience. Remember, there is no righteousness in this earth except Christ's righteousness. Ellen White wrote, "The only defense against evil is the indwelling Christ in the heart through faith in His righteousness" (*The Desire of Ages,* p. 324).

Personal Reflection and Discussion

1. What is Satan constantly trying to do in relation to Christ?

_____

_____

2. When we work hard to obey God in an attempt to be righteous, whose plan are we following?

_____

_____

3. What kind of life did Jesus live in relation to God's law?

_____

_____

4. According to the Bible, how can we be righteous?

_____

_____

5. How do we obtain righteousness?

_____

_____

Prayer Activity

- Call your prayer partner and discuss this devotional with him/her.
- Pray with your prayer partner:
    1. for God to baptize you with His Holy Spirit.
    2. for God to revive you and His church.
    3. for God to forgive you for seeking to be righteous by your own efforts.
    4. for God to lead you to understand and experience righteousness by faith in Christ alone.
    5. for the individuals on your prayer list.

Day 35

Thank You for the Thorns

When we understand righteousness by faith in Christ alone, we will come to the point where we can thank God for the thorns of temptation He allows to come to us. Paul understood this when he wrote:

"And lest I should be exalted above measure by the abundance of the revelations, a thorn in the flesh was given to me, a messenger of Satan to buffet me, lest I be exalted above measure. Concerning this thing I pleaded with the Lord three times that it might depart from me. And He said to me, 'My grace is sufficient for you, for My strength is made perfect in weakness.' Therefore most gladly I will rather boast in my infirmities, that the power of Christ may rest upon me. Therefore I take pleasure in infirmities, in reproaches, in needs, in persecutions, in distresses, for Christ's sake. For when I am weak, then I am strong" (2 Cor. 12:7-10).

Many things can be thorns in the flesh. Paul lists some of his thorns: infirmities, reproaches, necessities, persecutions, distresses. Paul prayed for God to remove them. But God said no. Why? God's grace was all Paul needed in order to deal with the thorns.

God also gave Paul a very important truth to remember and to share with others when He said, "My strength is made perfect in weakness." The weaker we know we are, the sooner we stop trying to exert our puny strength to overcome a thorny temptation in our life. Then the sooner we will begin experiencing God's mighty power in our life. Our own exertion of effort to overcome a temptation actually gets in the way of God's power to deliver. You see, when we do that we are looking to our strength and ability to overcome even though we think we are also depending on God

to "help" us. God wants to do much more than "help" us. He is the victory. Christ is our deliverance from temptation. When we back off from such efforts and get ourselves out of the way, then Christ can begin manifesting Himself in and through us. You have probably heard the saying, "Let go and let God." This is what that saying means.

This is why the Lord will leave some thorns of temptation in your life. I am sure you have prayed for God to remove thorns of besetting sins. They have brought discouragement and defeat in your life. However, God leaves them because He wants you to learn the lesson that His strength is made perfect in your weakness. When you begin experiencing Christ's deliverance in you then you, along with Paul, will declare, "Therefore most gladly I will rather boast in my infirmities, that the power of Christ may rest upon me. Therefore I take pleasure in infirmities, in reproaches, in needs, in persecutions, in distresses, for Christ's sake. For when I am weak, then I am strong."

You will come to the point that you actually thank God for the thorns in your life. Why? It is because of them that you came to experience the amazing delivering power of Christ. Because of them Christ has become even more precious to you. As He gives you the victory over your temptations, your praises for Him fill your heart.

You also rejoice in the thorns because they are opportunities for God's glory to shine forth through you as Christ manifests His life in and through you. They are opportunities for you to become more and more like Christ in those areas of your life as He manifests Himself more and more in your life.

This is what James was speaking of when he wrote: "My brethren, count it all joy when you fall into various trials, knowing that the testing of your faith produces patience [endurance]. But let patience have its perfect work, that you may be perfect and complete, lacking nothing" (James 1:2-4).

You will then experience what Paul describes "as sorrowful, yet always rejoicing" (2 Cor. 6:10). Even in the midst of the most difficult circumstances you will be able to rejoice because Jesus is manifesting Himself in you. Your faith in Christ develops an endurance that will lead to Christ manifesting Himself in you fully. During this process, you will become ready for His return.

Personal Reflection and Discussion

1. What did Paul realize about the thorns in his life?

_____

_____

2. Why does God not remove some temptations and trials in our life even though we ask Him to remove them?

_____

_____

3. Instead of trying hard to resist the temptation, how are we to obtain the victory over sin?

_____

_____

4. What do the thorns of temptation in your life enable Christ to do in your life?

_____

_____

5. How can Christians come to the place in their life where they can thank God for the thorns of temptation in their life?

_____

_____

Prayer Activity

- Call your prayer partner and discuss this devotional with him/her.
- Pray with your prayer partner:
    1. for God to baptize you with His Holy Spirit.
    2. for God to revive you and His church.
    3. for God to continue to lead you to understand and experience righteousness by faith in Christ alone.
    4. for Christ to manifest His victory when you are tempted.
    5. for the individuals on your prayer list.

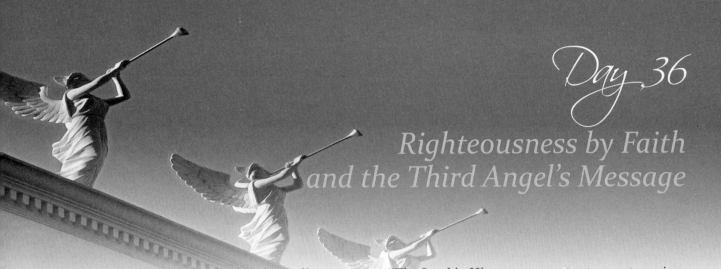

Righteousness by Faith and the Third Angel's Message

Righteousness by faith and the third angel's message are closely related. It is only through experiencing righteousness by faith in Christ alone that one will avoid being deceived by the last-day antichrist power.

Revelation 14 gives a serious warning about not worshipping the beast or antichrist: "Then a third angel followed them, saying with a loud voice, 'If anyone worships the beast and his image, and receives his mark on his forehead or on his hand, he himself shall also drink of the wine of the wrath of God, which is poured out full strength into the cup of His indignation'" (Rev. 14:9, 10).

The third angel's message calls men and women to obey God's commandments, including the fourth commandment, which admonishes us to keep holy the seventh-day Sabbath. The message includes a warning to all who turn from God and receive the "mark of the beast," which is Satan's counterfeit day of worship. Those who receive the mark of the beast will experience the seven last plagues and be lost (Rev. 14:9-11).

The purpose of the message of righteousness by faith in Christ is the same. Righteousness by faith leads men and women to obedience of God's commandments as they, in faith, allow Christ to live out His life of righteous obedience to God's law in their lives. Righteousness by faith leads to keeping God's commandments. This happens not by man's efforts but by faith in Christ to manifest His commandment–keeping in one's life.

Ellen White understood this when she wrote of God seeking to bring the message of righteousness by faith to the Seventh-day Adventist Church in 1888:

"The Lord in His great mercy sent a most precious message to His people through Elders Waggoner and Jones. This message was to bring more prominently before the world the uplifted Saviour, the sacrifice for the sins of the whole world. It presented justification through faith in the Surety; it invited the people to receive the righteousness of Christ, *which is made manifest in obedience to all the commandments of God*" (*Testimonies to Ministers and Gospel Workers*, pp. 91, 92, emphasis added).

She knew that reception of the message of righteousness by faith would lead to "obedience to all the commandments of God." Therefore, the message of righteousness by faith in Christ and the third angel's message are proclaimed to achieve the same goal—obedience to Gods' commandments.

The message of righteousness by faith must be proclaimed to the world as the third angel's message is proclaimed. This is necessary for the full gospel of a delivering Savior to be proclaimed, thus preparing a people for Christ's second coming. It is only as individuals understand and experience righteousness by faith in Christ alone that they will be able to remain faithful to God through the time of trouble and stand in the presence of Christ in all His glory at His return. It is only as righteousness by faith is understood and experienced that Jude's words will be true for us:

"Now to Him who is able to keep you from stumbling, and to present you faultless before the presence of His glory with exceeding joy, to God our Savior, who alone is wise, be glory and majesty, dominion and power, both now and forever. Amen" (Jude 24, 25).

Therefore, since the Seventh-day Adventist Church was raised up by God to give the last warning message to the world in preparation for Christ's second coming, it is essential that the message of righteousness by faith be an integral part of our teaching and preaching. By proclaiming the warning of Revelation 14:9-11, we present prophetic facts of coming events. However, that alone will not give the hearers what they need in order to be ready for those final events. The message of righteousness by faith must also be proclaimed so they will learn how to let Christ live out His commandment–keeping in and through them. Otherwise, their obedience will actually turn into legalism, because they will be seeking to keep God's commandments through their own efforts, which is a meritorious, legalistic obedience. When righteousness by faith is understood and experienced, Christ is actually doing the obedience in the life. Therefore, Christ alone gets the glory:

"That no flesh should glory in His presence. But of Him you are in Christ Jesus, who became for us wisdom from God—and righteousness and sanctification and redemption—that, as it is written, 'He who glories, let him glory in the Lord'" (1 Cor. 1:29-31).

Personal Reflection and Discussion

1. What serious warning does God give to the world in the third angel's message of Revelation 14?

_____

_____

2. What does that warning call the inhabitants of the world to do?

_____

_____

3. How is righteousness by faith closely related to this third angel's message?

_____

_____

4. How does understanding and experiencing righteousness by faith in Christ enable God's children to be ready for Christ's second coming?

_____

_____

Prayer Activity

- Call your prayer partner and discuss this devotional with him/her.
- Pray with your prayer partner:
    1. for God to baptize you with His Holy Spirit.
    2. for God to revive you and His church.
    3. for God to write His law on your heart.
    4. for Christ to live out His life of victory in your life.
    5. for the individuals on your prayer list.

Day 37

Righteousness by Faith and the Last Generation

Seventh-day Adventists have always had what might be called a "last–generation theology." This theology teaches that the last generation of Christians who are living when Jesus comes will have to have developed a relationship with Christ as no other generation before them. This will be necessary because they will have to be faithful to God through the time of trouble and stand in the presence of Christ in all His glory at His return. God's faithful followers will not be consumed while, all other inhabitants of earth will be destroyed by the brightness of His coming. It is only those who understand and experience righteousness by faith who will be able to endure these final events successfully.

The work of the Holy Spirit is essential for Christ to manifest Himself in His people. Christ lives in His children through the baptism of the Holy Spirit. Therefore, it is absolutely necessary for the last generation of believers to understand and experience the baptism of the Holy Spirit. Of this Ellen White wrote:

"Nothing but the baptism of the Holy Spirit can bring up the church to its right position, and prepare the people of God for the fast approaching conflict" (Manuscript Releases, vol. 2, p. 30).

She is very clear that receiving the baptism of the Holy Spirit is our only hope of being faithful to God during earth's final conflict.

According to the book of Revelation, the church is in a dangerous condition today. To this church God warns, "I know your works, that you are neither cold nor hot. I could wish you were cold or hot. So then, because you are lukewarm, and neither cold nor hot, I will [vomit] you out of My mouth. Because you say, 'I am rich, have become wealthy, and have need of noth-ing'—and do not know that you are wretched, miser-able, poor, blind, and naked" (Rev. 3:15-17). The church is described by God as being "lukewarm." If the church's condition doesn't change, she will be rejected by God: "I will [vomit] you out of My mouth."

Therefore, before Jesus returns the church must go through a major spiritual transformation. She must experience genuine revival and reformation. Ellen White understood this great need when she wrote:

"A revival of true godliness among us is the greatest and most urgent of all our needs. To seek this should be our first work" (Selected Messages, book. 1, p. 121).

There are two things necessary for revival to take place: prayer and the baptism of the Holy Spirit. Ellen White pointed this out in the following statements:

"A revival need be expected only in answer to prayer" (Ibid.).

"The baptism of the Holy Ghost as on the day of Pentecost will lead to a revival of true religion and the performance of many wonderful works" (Selected Messages, book. 2, p. 57).

As God's people personally experience the daily baptism of the Holy Spirit, Jesus will live in them. He will begin to manifest Himself in their lives. It is essential that they understand and experience righteousness by faith in order to understand how to let Jesus live out His life of victory over every temptation and sin in their life. This last generation must live a life of complete victory over all temptation and sin, which is only possible through Christ living in them.

Therefore, before the final events there will be a purifying work taking place in the hearts and lives of God's children who respond to God's call to be part of that last generation. The prophet Malachi referred to this time of purification in Malachi 3:1-4:

"'Behold, I send My messenger, and he will prepare the way before Me. And the Lord, whom you seek, will suddenly come to His temple, even the Messenger of the covenant, in whom you delight. Behold, He is coming,' says the Lord of hosts. 'But who can endure the day of His coming? And who can stand when He appears? For He is like a refiner's fire and like fullers' soap. He will sit as a refiner and a purifier of silver; He will purify the sons of Levi, and purge them as gold and silver, that they may offer to the Lord an offering in righteousness. Then the offering of Judah and Jerusalem will be pleasant to the Lord, as in the days of old, as in former years.'"

Notice several very important points in this statement. The prophet Malachi foretold a time just prior to Christ's second coming when a great refining process would take place among God's people. This purifying process will cause God's children to have spotless characters. They will have to be conquerors over every temptation and sin in their lives. This can happen only by daily receiving the baptism of the Holy Spirit and experiencing righteousness by faith in Christ alone.

Personal Reflection and Discussion

1. What two experiences must God's people have in order to be ready for Christ's second coming?
_____
_____

2. What did Ellen White say was our greatest need?
_____
_____

3. What two things bring revival to God people?
_____
_____

4. What did the prophet Malachi say God would do among His people just before Christ returns?
_____
_____

5. How can God's people experience this purification?
_____
_____

Prayer Activity

- Call your prayer partner and discuss this devotional with him/her.
- Pray with your prayer partner:
    1. for God to baptize you with His Holy Spirit.
    2. for God to revive you and His church.
    3. for God to purify you, as Malachi described, through experiencing righteousness by faith in Christ.
    4. for the individuals on your prayer list.

A People Blessed by the Early and Latter Rain of the Holy Spirit

Those who make it victoriously through the time of trouble and are ready for Christ's second coming are those who grow to full spiritual maturity under the early rain and latter rain of the Holy Spirit. The early rain of the Spirit began to fall on the day of Pentecost and has been available to every Christian since that day. When we seek the baptism of the Holy Spirit, we are actually seeking the early rain experience of the Spirit.

It is vital for us to daily experience the early rain baptism of the Holy Spirit in order to spiritually grow to the point where we will benefit from the latter rain of the Spirit, which prepares Christians for the final crisis and Christ's return. However, many don't realize this fact and feel they must wait for the latter rain of the Spirit in order finally to have the victory over their besetting sins and spiritual immaturity. Such a view will end in disaster for the one who holds to it. Ellen White warns us:

"I saw that many were neglecting the preparation so needful, and were looking to the time of 'refreshing' and the 'latter rain' to fit them to stand in the day of the Lord, and to live in His sight. Oh, how many I saw in the time of trouble without a shelter! They had neglected the needful preparation; therefore they could not receive the refreshing that all must have to fit them to live in the sight of a holy God" (*Christian Experience and Teachings of Ellen G. White*, p. 112).

We must have victory over all temptation and sin in our life if we are to benefit from the latter rain and the outpouring of the Spirit. If we believe we do not have to take seriously the sin problem in our lives, we are deceived by Satan. Ellen White confirms this with these words:

"I saw that none could share the 'refreshing' unless they obtained the victory over every besetment, over pride, selfishness, love of the world, and over every wrong word and action" (*Ibid.*, p. 113).

Peter confirmed this when he said, "Repent therefore and be converted, that your sins may be blotted out, so that times of refreshing may come from the presence of the Lord" (Acts 3:19).

The early or former rain of the Spirit, which is the baptism of the Holy Spirit, brings us to the spiritual maturity required in order to benefit from the latter rain.

"The latter rain, ripening earth's harvest, represents the spiritual grace that prepares the church for the coming of the Son of man. But unless the former rain has fallen, there will be no life; the green blade will not spring up. Unless the early showers have done their work, the latter rain can bring no seed to perfection" (*The Faith I Live By*, p. 333).

Full spiritual growth under the early rain baptism of the Spirit is necessary for us even to be able to recognize the latter rain of the Spirit when it falls.

"Unless we are daily advancing in the exemplification of the active Christian virtues, we shall not recognize the manifestation of the Holy Spirit in the latter rain. It may be falling on hearts all around us, but we shall not discern or receive it" (*Testimonies to Ministers and Gospel Workers*, p. 507).

This is why the Lord is calling His children to daily receive the baptism of the Holy Spirit now and come out of their Laodicean condition. We are fast approaching the time of the full outpouring of the latter rain of the Spirit. God is giving us a merciful call or warning to prepare for this final worldwide Holy Spirit

event. Only those who heed His call will receive the latter rain and be ready for Christ's coming. At that time they will be like Jesus: "Beloved, now we are children of God; and it has not yet been revealed what we shall be, but we know that when He is revealed, we shall be like Him, for we shall see Him as He is" (1 John 3:2).

Those who do not experience the early and latter rain will be like those on the day of Pentecost who did not receive the initial outpouring of the early rain. They will not understand what is happening and will mock those who are experiencing the fullness of God's power under these two great outpourings of the Holy Spirit.

Personal Reflection and Discussion

1. When did the early rain of the Spirit begin?

_____

_____

2. What must happen under the early rain baptism of the Holy Spirit in order to benefit from the latter rain?

_____

_____

3. If we are waiting for the latter rain of the Spirit to give us the victory over temptation and sin, what will be our fate?

_____

_____

4. What does the early rain baptism of the Spirit and latter rain of the Spirit prepare the Christian for?

_____

_____

Prayer Activity

- Call your prayer partner and discuss this devotional with him/her.
- Pray with your prayer partner:
    1. for God to baptize you with His Holy Spirit.
    2. for God to revive you and His church.
    3. for God to lead you to grow in spiritual maturity under the early rain of the Spirit in order to benefit from the latter rain.
    4. for the individuals on your prayer list.

Day 39

A People of Prayer and Fasting

Those ready to meet Jesus will be a people who pray and fast. They will follow the example of Jesus in every way, including Jesus' prayer life. Jesus began His ministry with 40 days of prayer and fasting. At times He spent entire nights in prayer. Prayer was necessary for Him to stay connected with His Father and be strengthened for His daily conflicts with Satan.

Before Jesus entered into the 40 days of prayer and fasting, He was filled with the Spirit as an answer to prayer at His water baptism: "When all the people were baptized, it came to pass that Jesus also was baptized; and while He prayed, the heaven was opened. And the Holy Spirit descended in bodily form like a dove upon Him, and a voice came from heaven which said, 'You are My beloved Son; in You I am well pleased'" (Luke 3:21, 22). The baptism of the Holy Spirit was a major factor in Jesus' spiritual life

The same will be true of those ready for Christ's return. They will be a Spirit-filled people who have a consistent, powerful prayer life. They will have this kind of prayer life because they will be filled with God's Spirit, which is also the Spirit of intercession: "And I will pour on the house of David and on the inhabitants of Jerusalem the Spirit of grace and supplication" (Zech. 12:10). It is the Holy Spirit that keeps giving them the desire to pray. In fact, the Spirit calls them to pray, directs their prayers, gives them faith, and empowers their prayers. In short, they continuously pray in the Spirit as Paul counsels: "Praying always with all prayer and supplication in the Spirit, being watchful to this end with all perseverance and supplication for all the saints" (Eph. 6:18).

Charles Finney, the well-known nineteenth century revivalist/evangelist, said:

"If you would pray in faith, be sure to walk every day with God. If you do, He will tell you what to pray for. Be filled with His Spirit, and He will give you objects enough to pray for. He will give you as much of the spirit of prayer as you have strength of body to bear" (*Sermons on Gospel Themes*, pp. 56, 57).

God's last-day remnant people know that prayer releases the power of God. Because of this, they view prayer as a necessity in their personal life and in the advancement of God's work. They know that from the beginning God intended to work through man and not independent of him in carrying out His will on earth. They know that when God wills to do something on earth He impresses His people to pray for that very thing. Many statements by Jesus confirm this truth. In the Lord's Prayer Jesus told us to pray that "Your will be done on earth as it is in heaven" (Matt. 6:10). When He saw so many people suffering, He felt compassion for them and told us to "pray the Lord of the harvest to send out laborers into His harvest" (Matt. 9:38).

Those ready to meet Jesus will also be a people who fast. When Jesus said "When you fast" (Matt. 6:16), He was directing His disciples to take time to fast. Ellen White supported the importance of fasting when she wrote:

"Now and onward till the close of time the people of God should be more earnest, more wide-awake, not trusting in their own wisdom, but in the wisdom of their Leader. They should set aside days for fasting and prayer. Entire abstinence from food may not be required, but they should eat sparingly of the most simple food" (*Counsels on Diet and Food*, pp. 188, 189).

"We cannot have a weak faith now; we cannot be safe in a listless, indolent, slothful attitude. Every jot of ability is to be used, and sharp, calm, deep thinking is to be done. The wisdom of any human agent is not sufficient for the planning and devising in this time. Spread every plan before God with fasting, and with the humbling of the soul before the Lord Jesus, and commit thy ways unto the Lord" (*Selected Messages*, book 2, p. 364).

Those ready to meet Jesus will be a people who pray and fast. These actions will play a major role in strengthening their relationship with God, increasing their faith, clarifying God's will for their life and ministry, and making their ministry effective in finishing God's work. If you want to be among God's last-day remnant people who are ready to meet Jesus, you must become a Spirit-filled man or woman, who consistently prays and fasts on a regular basis. This is God's ordained way—the only way. There are no other options.

Personal Reflection and Discussion

1. What kind of prayer life did Jesus have?

_____

_____

2. What does the baptism of the Holy Spirit do for the Christian's prayer life?

_____

_____

3. Why is prayer necessary for God's will to be carried out?

_____

_____

4. Why is fasting important in the Christian's life?

_____

_____

Prayer Activity

- Call your prayer partner and discuss this devotional with him/her.
- Pray with your prayer partner:
    1. for God to baptize you with His Holy Spirit.
    2. for God to revive you and His church.
    3. for God to lead you to pray and fast in the Spirit.
    4. for the individuals on your prayer list.

Those who make it through the time of trouble and are ready to meet Jesus will definitely be a people grounded in the Word of God. The Bible will have played a major role in enlightening them concerning God's will and strengthening them for the final conflict. They will have learned the truth that "man shall not live by bread alone, but by every word that proceeds from the mouth of God" (Matt. 4:4).

God's people will not become fearful of what Satan might do to them. As we studied earlier, fear is the opposite of faith and gives Satan a right of passage into our life in the very area we fear. Instead of fear, we must put our complete trust in God's Word. Remember, "faith is not believing God can. Faith is knowing God will."

God's last-day people will have the confidence expressed by John: "Now this is the confidence that we have in Him, that if we ask anything according to His will, He hears us. And if we know that He hears us, whatever we ask, we know that we have the petitions that we have asked of Him" (1 John 5:14, 15).

In order for us to have this kind of faith, we must become familiar with God's Word. It must become our meditation day and night (Joshua 1:8). Then our ways will be prosperous and victorious. We will be like a "tree planted by the rivers of water, that brings forth its fruit in its season" (Ps. 1:2, 3).

God's Word is to play a major role in our victories over temptation and sin. It does more than simply inform us concerning what sin is, "I would not have known sin except through the law. For I would not have known covetousness unless the law had said, "You shall not covet" (Rom. 7:7). It is by faith in the promise of the Bible that we obtain victory.

Paul calls the Word of God the "sword of the Spirit" (Eph. 6:17). The Greek word translated "word" in this verse is *rhema*, which means spoken word. Therefore, the Word of God spoken in faith will bring the changes in our life that are necessary for us to become like Jesus in character and ministry. Jesus spoke of this when He said, "For assuredly, I say to you, whoever says to this mountain, 'Be removed and be cast into the sea,' and does not doubt in his heart, but believes that those things he says will be done, he will have whatever he says" (Mark 11:23).

Notice that Jesus strongly emphasized the importance of "saying" what we believe will happen. When we speak the will of God as revealed in His Word and believe what we say, it will come to pass in our life. Speaking the Word of God in faith is a very powerful weapon.

Ellen White wrote of the power of God's Word:

"The creative energy that called the worlds into existence is in the word of God. This word imparts power; it begets life. Every command is a promise; accepted by the will, received into the soul, it brings with it the life of the Infinite One. It transforms the nature and re-creates the soul in the image of God.

"The life thus imparted is in like manner sustained. 'By every word that proceedeth out of the mouth of God' (Matt. 4:4)" (*Education*, p. 126).

There is no shortage of power to transform us into the image of Christ. Faith in God's promises brings the Holy Spirit's power into our life. When we learn how to exercise the weapons of our warfare, we will then be able to pull down every stronghold Satan has in our life, whether spiritual, emotional, or physical.

"For the weapons of our warfare are not carnal but mighty in God for pulling down strongholds, casting down arguments and every high thing that exalts itself against the knowledge of God, bringing every thought into captivity to the obedience of Christ" (2 Cor. 10:4, 5).

Remember, just before Jesus comes Satan's decep-tions will be very effective in leading multitudes away from God and causing them to be lost when Jesus comes. The deceptions will be so powerful that, if it were possible, the very elect will be deceived (Matt. 24:24). Understanding and accepting the Word of God is essential in order to avoid the deceptions of the last days.

Personal Reflection and Discussion

1. Why is the Word of God, the Bible, so important for the Christian?

_____

_____

2. What did Paul call the Word of God?

_____

_____

3. How did Ellen White describe God's Word?

_____

_____

4. How does God's Word help us to avoid Satan's last-day deceptions?

_____

_____

5. What part does God's Word play in your life?

_____

_____

Prayer Activity

- **Call your prayer partner and discuss this devotional with him/her.**
- **Pray with your prayer partner:**
    1. **for God to baptize you with His Holy Spirit.**
    2. **for God to revive you and His church.**
    3. **for God to put in your heart the desire to study His Word more.**
    4. **for the individuals on your prayer list.**

After 40 Days of Prayer and Devotional Studies . . .

Now that you have completed the 40 days of prayer and devotional studies, you probably don't want the experience you are having with the Lord and the fellowship you are enjoying to fade away. So, what should you do next?

If you haven't studied the first 40–days devotional book, *40 Days—Prayers and Devotions to Prepare for the Second Coming,* I would suggest you begin that daily study.

Another possibility is that you begin studying in greater detail the subjects presented in this devotional and the first 40-day devotional book. Each section has been based on several of the books I have written. The titles of the books are:

- *The Baptism of the Holy Spirit*

- *Spirit Baptism and Evangelism*

- *Spirit Baptism and Abiding in Christ*

- *Spirit Baptism and Waiting on God*

- *Spirit Baptism and Christ's Glorious Return*

- *Spirit Baptism and the 1888 Message of Righteousness by Faith*

- *Spirit Baptism and Prayer*

- *Spirit Baptism and Earth's Final Events*

- *Spirit Baptism and New Wineskin Fellowship*

- *Spirit Baptism and Deliverance*

Second, continue to pray for those on your prayer list and reach out to them. Also, add others to your list as the Lord leads, and as a group consider activities to plan to invite those on the prayer lists to attend.

Christ wants personal daily devotional study, prayer, and reaching out to others to become an integral part of every Christian's life. If this aspect of your life ends with the 40 days of prayer and devotional study, you will not grow into the fullness of Christ that He desires you to experience. Also, this is the only way to be ready for Christ's soon return. For it is the only way our intimate relationship with Christ develops and grows. May the Lord abundantly bless your continued devotional study and prayer time with Him, and your efforts to share Him with others.

Note: All books listed are available through most Adventist Book Centers or at www.40daysdevotional.com.

SUPERPOWER RIVALRY

RELATIONS BETWEEN THE
UNITED STATES AND
THE SOVIET UNION
1945-91

LAURA KWASNIEWSKA

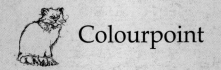

Colourpoint

8 7 6 5 4 3 2

© Laura Kwasniewska
Newtownards
1997

ISBN (Higher level) 1 898392 35 8

Layout and design: Colourpoint Books
Maps: Norman Johnston
Printed by: ColourBooks

Acknowledgements:
Associated Press, Topham: Cover (right), 17 (bottom),
20, 21, 25, 32 (left); Daily Mail: 34 (right); Mirror
Syndication International: Cover (left), 28, 41 (top
right); Punch magazine: 12 (right), 13, 17 (top); Ron
Haeberle © Life Magazine/Time Inc: 41 (bottom
right); Sunday Times: 7 (both); Time Life - Colorific!:
47; Topham Picture Point: 6 (lower), 11, 32 (right),
33, 36, 39, 41 (top left, middle right, bottom left), 43,
50, 57, 59 (top); United Artists (courtesy Kobal): 30;
US Army: 41 (middle left).

Every effort has been made to trace the copyright
owners of all pictures used. If there are any
inadvertent ommissions, the publisher apologises and
will be only too happy to come to a suitable
accommodation.

COLOURPOINT BOOKS
Unit D5, Ards Business Centre
Jubilee Road
NEWTOWNARDS
Co Down
BT23 4YH
Tel: (028) 9182 0505
Fax: (028) 9182 1900
E-mail: info@colourpoint.co.uk
Web site: www.colourpoint.co.uk

The Author: Laura Kwasniewska, who was awarded
her Master's degree in 1986, is an experienced teacher
of history and head of department. She is currently
seconded to the Western Education and Library Board
as advisory teacher for history.

CHRONOLOGY

1945	Feb	Yalta Conference
	July/Aug	Potsdam Conference
	Aug	Atomic bombs dropped on Hiroshima and Nagasaki
1946	Mar	Churchill's 'Iron Curtain' speech
1947	Mar	Truman Doctrine
	June	Marshall Plan announced
	Sept	Cominform set up
1948	Feb	Communists seize power in Czechoslovakia
	June	Berlin Blockade begins
1949	Jan	Comecon set up
	April	NATO established
	May	End of Berlin Blockade. Federal Republic of Germany (West Germany) set up
	Aug	USSR explodes atom bomb
	Oct	People's Republic of China proclaimed
		German Democratic Republic (East Germany) set up
1950	June	Korean War begins
1951	Sept	USA, Australia and New Zealand sign ANZUS Pact
1952	Nov	US explodes H-bomb
1953	Mar	Death of Stalin
	July	End of Korean War
	Aug	USSR explodes H-bomb
1954	July	Vietnam divided along 17th parallel
	Sept	SEATO established
1955	May	West Germany joins NATO Warsaw Pact formed
1956	Feb	Khrushchev denounces Stalin and calls for peaceful co-existence
	Oct	Hungarian Uprising
1957	Oct	USSR launches first Sputnik
1959	Jan	Castro seizes power in Cuba
1960	May	U2 incident
1961	April	Bay of Pigs landing in Cuba
	Aug	Berlin Wall built
1962	Oct	Cuban Missile Crisis
1963	June	Hot-Line Agreement

	Aug	Partial Nuclear Test Ban Treaty
	Nov	Kennedy assassinated
1964	Aug	Gulf of Tonkin incident
	Oct	Khrushchev replaced by Brezhnev
1965	Mar	Johnson sent troops to Vietnam
1968	Jan	Tet Offensive
		Dubcek became leader in Czechoslovakia
	Aug	Soviet invasion of Czechoslovakia
1971	Oct	China admitted to UN
1972	Feb	Nixon visits China
	May	Nixon visits Moscow SALT I signed
	Dec	East and West Germany sign Basic Treaty
1973	Jan	USA - N Vietnam ceasefire
1974	Aug	Nixon resigns after Watergate scandal
1975	Aug	Helsinki Agreement signed
1979	June	Carter and Brezhnev sign SALT II
	Dec	Soviet invasion of Afghanistan
1980	Aug	Solidarity founded in Poland
1982	June	Talks for START begin
	Nov	Death of Brezhnev
1983	Mar	Reagan announces SDI
	Nov	Cruise and Pershing missiles based in Europe
1985	Mar	Gorbachev becomes new Soviet leader
1987	Dec	INF Treaty signed
1989	Feb	Soviet troops withdraw from Afghanistan
	June	Solidarity wins Polish election
	Oct	End of communist rule in Hungary
	Nov	Berlin Wall taken down
	Dec	End of communist rule in East Germany, Czechoslovakia, Bulgaria and Romania
1990	Oct	East and West Germany united
1991	Jan	Gulf war begins
	Aug	START I signed
	Dec	Gorbachev resigns — end of USSR

1.1 WHAT ARE SUPERPOWERS?

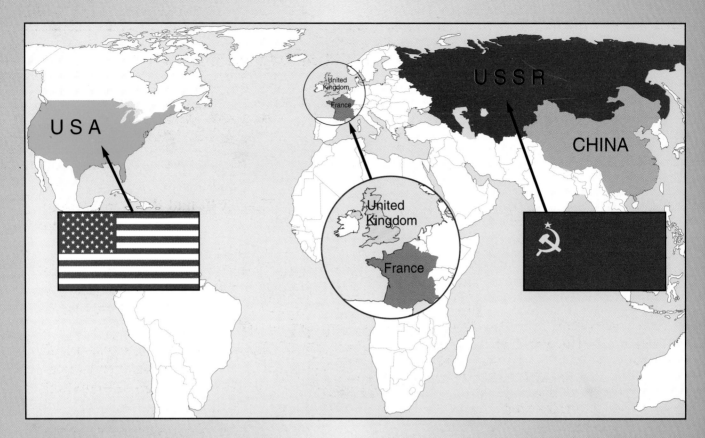

From the end of the Second World War in 1945, until 1990, world events were dominated by two countries — the Soviet Union (USSR) and the United States of America. Both were described as **superpowers**, a term which had come into use by 1945, to distinguish them from the traditional **great power** countries such as Britain and France.

Why were the USSR and USA called Superpowers?

1 Both had large populations, which meant they could raise large armies as well as expand their labour force in time of war.
2 Both were vast geographically and were rich in natural resources, which provided the raw material for war — eg coal and iron ore for the steel industry, oil for transport.
3 Both were victorious against Germany, whose armies had seemed unbeatable as recently as 1941.
4 Both would ultimately control huge arsenals of nuclear weapons. Though the United States (with British assistance) was the first to develop and use the atom bomb in 1945, the Soviet Union exploded its first atomic bomb in 1949. Its first hydrogen bomb was tested only months after the Americans' successful test in 1952.
5 While the USSR had the largest army in the world, with approximately six million men, 50,000 tanks and 20,000 aircraft, the United States was clearly the richest country in the world. Most European countries, including the USSR, had been invaded and suffered terrible damage to their cities and industries. The USA had escaped such ruin and, instead, the war had ended the Depression, provided full employment and opened new markets. By 1945 the USA had control of one third of the world's industrial production and half of the world's shipping. American wealth made D-day possible.
6 By contrast, their former enemies, Japan and Germany, were shattered by defeat; while their ally Britain was bankrupted by the long struggle for victory. France was recovering from the effects of a third German invasion in seventy five years.
7 In 1945 America and the Soviet Union had no rivals but each other. Only they had the will, the resources and the military power to take on a global role. Consequently, the peace and stability of the post-war world depended upon the relationship between the two superpowers.

How did the Superpowers dominate international affairs after 1945?

Military might and economic strength allowed the superpowers to dominate world events after

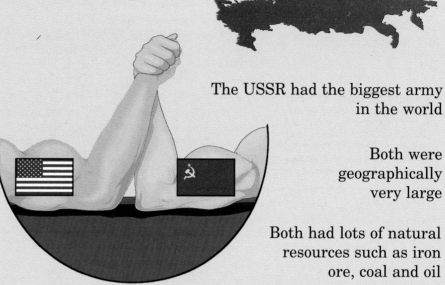

Why were the USA and the USSR called Superpowers?

The USA was very rich

Both had huge populations

Both had beaten Germany in the Second World War.

No other countries were big enough to challenge them

The USSR had the biggest army in the world

Both were geographically very large

Both had lots of natural resources such as iron ore, coal and oil

Both had nuclear weapons

1945. The USSR could control most of Eastern Europe because the Red Army occupied it, and the USA used the power of the dollar. Both could frighten or persuade weaker countries into becoming **satellites**, ie countries which supported one or other of the superpowers in return for protection, military aid or economic assistance. Each superpower and its satellites formed a **power bloc**, ie a group of friendly countries which tended to follow the lead of one superpower against the other.

Like gang leaders, the two superpowers depended upon their satellites, both for their own security and to demonstrate their power and influence. Satellites provided resources and support but expected rewards and favours in return. The relationship between superpower and satellite was, therefore, based upon mutual need and mutual exploitation.

After 1945 the world was divided into two blocs — the **Eastern Bloc** (Soviet) and the **Western Bloc** (American). No country was considered neutral or **non-aligned**, though by the 1960s the superpowers accepted that there was a **Third World** of non-aligned countries. As their satellites were so important to the superpowers,

both became nervous if a satellite showed signs of wanting to leave the **bloc**. In extreme cases they might use force to prevent this happening, as the USSR did in Hungary in 1956 and Czechoslovakia in 1968. Both superpowers were likely to support a satellite which became involved in a regional conflict. For example, the USA supported South Korea and South Vietnam. However the greatest threat to world peace arose when the two superpowers came into direct confrontation — as in Berlin in 1949 and Cuba in 1962 — or found themselves supporting different sides — as in the Middle East conflicts of 1967 and 1973.

While any direct confrontation between the superpowers threatened war on a vast scale, the fact that both possessed **nuclear weapons** after 1949 made such confrontations highly dangerous. The traditional **balance of power** system of the 19th century and early 20th century became instead a **balance of terror**. A nuclear war between the superpowers would destroy not only themselves and their satellites, but also neutral countries and possibly the whole world. Though the United States and Russia had never fought each other, the second half of the 20th century was dominated by the fear that they might do so and with terrible consequences for mankind.

It was the knowledge of their power to unleash mutual destruction which holds the key to understanding the **Cold War** after 1945. Whatever interests were threatened, neither superpower was prepared to use its most deadly weapons to annihilate its opponent, because, in doing so, it would only destroy itself.

Consequently the Cold War was fought by other and lesser means and, despite the tensions and crises, nuclear war was avoided.

A *cartoon showing the USA and USSR dividing the world.*

American atomic bomb being tested at Bikini Atoll.

?

1 (a) What point is the cartoonist making in source A?
(b) Do you agree with his representation of the world after 1945? Explain your answer.

2 What is the link between source B and the Cold War between the superpowers after 1945?

3 Why did the superpowers need satellites and what were the consequences for both?

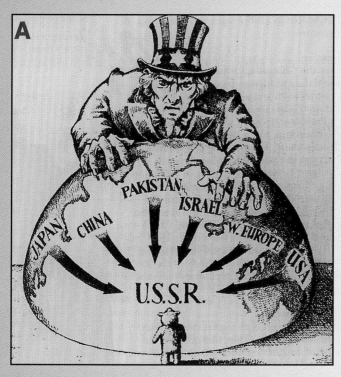

A Soviet view of the world.

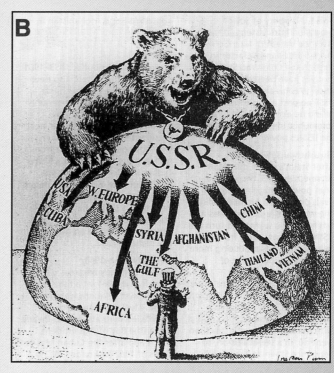

An American view of the world.

In the aftermath of war the Europe of 1945 was one of ill-defined borders and economic ruin. Both superpowers sought to reshape the world, but each had a different vision of the future. America and the Soviet Union had forged a wartime alliance of mutual convenience against the common enemy, Hitler's Germany. Once Germany was defeated they needed each other less and the fundamental differences between them resurfaced.

THE CAUSES OF RIVALRY

Ideology

There were huge differences between the two types of governments, economies and societies (see table, page 8). The United States made no secret of its hatred of **communism** and feared that Stalin wanted to expand communism, starting with Eastern Europe. The Soviet Union hated **capitalism** and believed it and communism could not co-exist. Mutual hatred of each other's ideology bred fear and mistrust and influenced actions as well as response.

1 The Americans timed the explosion of their first atomic bomb for 7 August 1945 — one day before the deadline (agreed at Yalta) when the Soviets would declare war on Japan. Thus America, not the USSR, was seen as the country which forced the Japanese to surrender.

2 The Americans only told Stalin about the atomic bomb at the **Potsdam** conference in 1945. Stalin was suspicious about their motive for secrecy and feared the US monopoly of this new and powerful weapon.

3 Stalin suspected that the Allies had deliberately delayed their invasion of France (the so-called **second front**) so that Germany and the USSR could exhaust each other. Consequently the extent of Soviet losses (estimated at 26 million) was blamed partly on the Allies' delay. Such suspicions were fuelled by memories of how both British and American troops had invaded the USSR in 1919-1920 to help the enemies of the communist government.

4 The Americans wanted to open up or revive European markets, including that of Germany, as quickly as possible after the war so as to boost world trade and maintain production and employment levels at home. This, they believed, was essential to their long-term economic security. However Stalin saw only that the United States was already the richest country in the world and that it appeared intent upon world domination via the dollar.

5 The Americans did not want to repeat the mistakes of 1919 and punish Germany too harshly. Stalin believed the Germans should pay for the damage they had done to the Soviet

7

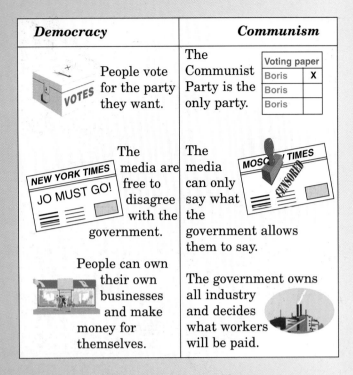

Democracy	Communism
People vote for the party they want.	The Communist Party is the only party.
	Voting paper Boris — X Boris — Boris —
The media are free to disagree with the government.	The media can only say what the government allows them to say.
People can own their own businesses and make money for themselves.	The government owns all industry and decides what workers will be paid.

• They represented opposing ideologies.

• They perceived each other as ambitious and eager to expand their influence. On the one hand Western powers feared that the Soviets were intent upon spreading communism, not only in countries under Soviet control but elsewhere (eg in Italy and France, where communist parties attracted increasing support). On the other hand the Soviets feared encirclement by capitalist states — hence Stalin's desire to control the neighbouring countries of Eastern Europe and to establish Soviet satellite states in the region.

• As both emerged from the war far stronger than any other nation, they saw each other as rivals and therefore as a threat. While the USSR retained the largest army in the world, the USA began a rapid demobilisation, cutting the armed forces from twelve to three million in a year. However Stalin could point to the US monopoly of the atomic bomb as adequate compensation for the reduction in troops.

• As both felt threatened they acted defensively to protect their interests and reinforced the impression that their intentions had always been aggressive.

• As part of their defensive strategy, both superpowers attempted to keep their plans and developments shrouded in secrecy. Both feared to admit fully to any current weakness or to any worries about their security in the future. Consequently, in 1945, the Americans over-estimated the strength of the USSR and failed to appreciate the seriousness of its economic problems so that before long they were displaying more sympathy for defeated Germany than for their recent ally, the Soviet Union.

Union in the war. After the invasions of 1914 and 1941 he was determined to prevent another. His tougher attitude towards Germany was interpreted by the Americans as evidence of the Soviet Union's determination to increase its own power at the expense of other countries. Before long the Americans were comparing Stalin to Hitler.

6 The Soviet Union may have emerged victorious from the war, but the appalling devastation filled her leaders with a strong sense of insecurity about the future. Ultimately they came to believe that their long term security depended upon weakening the US position, while the Americans were equally determined to limit what they saw as Soviet ambitions.

Perceptions

International relations, like personal relations, are strongly influenced by perceptions, ie how people see each other. When they conclude that another is unfriendly, over-ambitious and untrustworthy, their behaviour alters. They make assumptions about the other's intentions, expect the worst possible scenario, act accordingly and not surprisingly, often find their expectations are fulfilled. Similarly, government leaders and policy advisers in the USA and USSR constantly analysed each other's intentions and behaviour and expected the worst. Each had legitimate reasons to regard the other with suspicion:

?

1 Why did America and the Soviet Union distrust each other? List the reasons on both sides and complete a table like the one below:

Soviet reasons	American reasons

2 Compare sources A and B. In what ways do they agree and how do they differ?

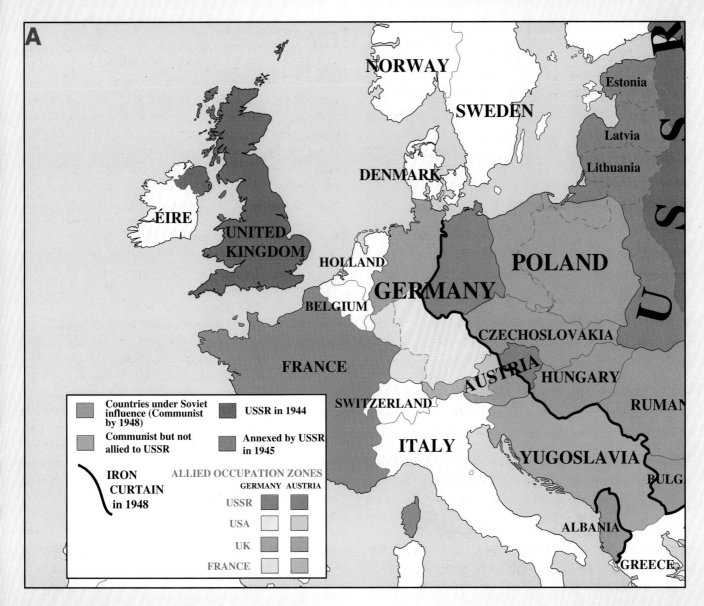

By the beginning of 1945 it was clear that the Allies were going to win the war. The German army was in retreat and, in anticipation of its final surrender the Allies needed to make decisions about the future of Europe as it emerged from the upheaval and devastation of war. For this reason the leaders of Britain, America and the Soviet Union held two major conferences in **1945** at **Yalta** and **Potsdam**. These conferences help explain how the wartime allies became divided in peace.

Yalta

In February at the Black Sea resort of Yalta, Winston Churchill, Franklin Roosevelt and Josef Stalin — the **Big Three** — agreed on a number of issues:
- The USSR would declare war on Japan three months after Germany surrendered.

- Germany and Austria would be divided into four zones of occupation (the British wanted France to have control of a zone as they believed that US troops would be withdrawn from Europe by 1947).
- Nazi war criminals would be punished.
- All three would join the new **United Nations Organisation** which would aim to keep the peace after the war. (Its charter was drawn up at a conference in San Francisco in April 1945.)
- Churchill and Roosevelt accepted that Eastern Europe would be a Soviet **sphere of influence**. This was to ease Soviet fears about their future security.
- In the **Declaration of Liberal Europe** the three leaders called for countries which were liberated to hold *"free elections of governments responsible to the will of the people"*.

9

In fact it is doubtful whether Roosevelt really believed that Stalin would permit free elections to be held in the countries of Eastern Europe which were first liberated and then controlled by the Red Army. However, because the American President placed a great deal of faith in the future role of the United Nations Organisation, decisions about the future of Europe were postponed until the war was over. By that time the Red Army had established firm control over Eastern Europe so that the Western allies would be unable to enforce their principle of democratically elected governments. As Stalin commented in April 1945:

"Whoever occupies territory also imposes his own social system as far as his army can reach. It cannot be otherwise."

At Yalta the allies could not agree about Poland. Churchill reminded them that Britain had declared war on Germany in September 1939 because Hitler had invaded Poland. Hence Britain wanted to create a free and independent Poland, but the USSR, which had taken advantage of Hitler's aggression to invade and occupy much of Poland, was more concerned with its own security. In July 1944 the Red Army had set up a Polish Communist government in Lublin and in the following October stood by while Nazis crushed the Warsaw uprising. Stalin argued:

"For Russia, it is not only a question of honour, but security — not only because we are on Poland's frontier, but also because throughout history Poland has always been a corridor for attack on Russia."

In order to protect the Soviet Union Stalin wanted a friendly (ie communist) Polish government and he wanted to regain land lost to Poland in 1920. In return, Poland would take part of east Germany — thus the whole country would be moved westwards. Though Churchill disapproved, he persuaded Roosevelt to agree, in return for Stalin's non-interference in Greece, where the British were supporting the monarchy against the communists. Poland's new boundaries were agreed at Yalta but despite promises no free elections were held.

Potsdam

The second conference of 1945 took place at Potsdam, near Berlin in July-August. Roosevelt had died in April 1945 so it was his successor, **President Harry Truman** who represented America. During the conference Churchill lost

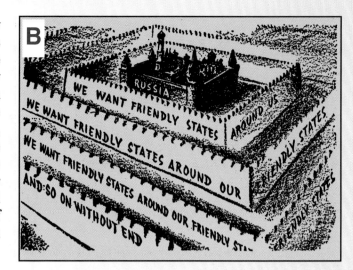

An American cartoon.

the general election and **Clement Attlee**, the new Labour Prime Minister, replaced him. Truman was more impatient than Roosevelt. He spoke in plain (and often undiplomatic) language to the Soviets and, after VE Day, abruptly ended America's **Lend-Lease** aid to the USSR. He was suspicious of Stalin's intentions and took a tough line with him, possibly because he knew America had the advantage of the **atomic bomb**. Its first successful test was carried out on **16 July 1945** the day before the conference opened. Truman mentioned the new weapon to Stalin, but did not explain how powerful it was.

At this conference the allies disagreed about Germany's future and especially about how much compensation (**reparations**) it should pay. Some decisions were taken:

- Germany would be disarmed.
- Leading Nazis would be put on trial for war crimes.
- An **Allied Control Council** would administer the four zones of military occupation (Berlin was also divided into four zones) but as **General de Gaulle** of France had vetoed moves to treat Germany as a whole, each power was free to pursue its own policy in the area under its control.
- Each occupying power could take reparations from its own zone. The USSR could also take 25% of all manufactured goods, especially machinery, from the other zones but, in return, was expected to supply them with food, coal and raw materials.

During the discussions on reparations it became clear that the USSR wanted to extract huge reparations to pay for its own economic

C

THE COLD WAR WAS THE BRAVE AND ESSENTIAL RESPONSE OF FREE MEN TO COMMUNIST AGGRESSION. THE WEST WAS FACED AT THE END OF THE SECOND WORLD WAR WITH A RELENTLESS DRIVE FOR DOMINATION BY THE SOVIET UNION. IN THE END, NOTHING COULD SATISIFY STALIN'S PARANOIA. HIS OWN ADVISERS FAILED TO DO SO. WHY DOES ANYONE SUPPOSE THAT ANY AMERICAN POLICY COULD HAVE DONE SO?

From **The Origins of the Cold War** by A M Schlesinger, 1967.

D

STALIN PREFERRED TO CONCENTRATE ON HIS OWN SPHERE. HIS MOST PROVOCATIVE ACTIONS, LIKE THE BERLIN BLOCKADE, WERE REACTIONS TO THE TRUMAN DOCTRINE, THE MARSHALL PLAN AND WESTERN POLICY IN GERMANY. THERE IS, THEN, REASON TO GIVE AS MUCH OF THE RESPONSIBILITY FOR THE ORIGINS OF THE COLD WAR TO THE USA AS TO THE SOVIET UNION. BUT THE CAUSES OF THE COLD WAR WERE MORE COMPLICATED. THE USA WAS RESPONDING TO A RANGE OF WHAT IT SAW AS DANGERS. AMERICAN POLICIES WERE AN ATTEMPT TO COPE WITH THE RESULTS OF THE SECOND WORLD WAR AS MUCH AS A RESPONSE TO THE SOVIET SYSTEM.

From **A Preponderance of Power** by M Leffler, 1992.

Churchill, Truman and Stalin at the Potsdam Conference , July 1945.

recovery. The Western allies feared this would only cripple Germany and force them to provide economic aid. The decision not to treat Germany as a single economic unit limited the drain on its resources but ultimately paved the way for the long-term division of the country.

The gulf widens

By January 1946 Truman was clearly exasperated with the Soviets when he wrote:

"Unless Russia is faced with an iron fist and strong language another war is in the making. Only one language do they understand — 'How many divisions have you got?'... I'm tired of babying the Soviets" (Letter to James Byrnes, Secretary of State 5 Jan 1945.)

Mistrust had deepened for a number of reasons:

1 The explosion of the world's first atomic bomb in Hiroshima in August 1945 altered the balance of power in America's favour and made the Soviets feel threatened. Not surprisingly, an American attempt to achieve a permanent monopoly of atomic weapons failed in 1946.

2 By 1946 the Soviet Union, in pursuit of security, had installed communist governments in Poland, Romania, Bulgaria and Albania, none of which had strong communist parties in 1945. There were no free elections, as promised at Yalta, and the spread of communism in Europe made Western leaders feel threatened. In February 1946 Stalin spoke of the inevitability of war with capitalist countries and said that the USSR had to embark on three more Five Year Plans.

3 In March 1946 at Fulton, Missouri, Churchill spoke of an **'iron curtain'** from the Baltic to the Adriatic, behind which lay countries "subject to a very high and increasing measure of control from Moscow" (source F). Stalin angrily defended the Soviet Union's need for friendly states as neighbours.

4 Fear of Soviet expansion made the British and Americans apply pressure for the withdrawal of Soviet troops from Iran, which had been a

F

A British cartoon about Churchill, titled 'A peep under the Iron Curtain'.

G

This British cartoon of June 1947 shows Truman and Stalin as rival bus drivers attracting custom to their hotels.

target for Russian expansion since the 19th century and lay within reach of the Middle East oil fields.

5 Both countries engaged in a war of propaganda where each other's actions were presented to the public in the worst possible light. This deepened suspicion and made it more widespread (sourceB and G).

6 The Soviets failed to supply the Western zones with food as agreed so, in May 1946, the USA stopped the removal of reparations from their zone, much to the annoyance of the USSR.

7 In July 1946 the USSR offered to create a centralised, united Germany and the USA responded in September with promises of a federal, democratic government and economic recovery.

Different priorities drove a wedge between the superpowers and distrust, the legacy of the past, pulled them apart. At this point George Kennan, an American diplomat based in Moscow, wrote an analysis of Soviet intentions which made American policy makers review their position. Kennan believed that the Soviet Union would never live in harmony with the West. Its strong sense of insecurity combined with its Marxist ideology would force it to be expansionist and therefore hostile. Kennan recommended that the

US should do everything in its power to **contain** the Soviet Union within its sphere of influence (ie confine it to its present position). And so the policy of **containment** was born.

?

1 How did American and Soviet policy differ in relation to (a) Eastern Europe and (b) Germany?

2 What did Churchill mean by an 'iron curtain'?

3 How reliable are sources B and G as historical evidence? Explain your answer.

4 Read sources C and D. What is the main difference between them when explaining the origins of the Cold War?

1.4 Truman and the Policy of Containment

A

LIKE APPLES IN A BARREL INFECTED BY A ROTTEN ONE, THE CORRUPTION OF GREECE WOULD ALSO CARRY INFECTION TO AFRICA, THROUGH ASIA MINOR AND EGYPT AND TO EUROPE THROUGH ITALY AND FRANCE, ALREADY THREATENED BY THE STRONGEST DOMESTIC COMMUNIST PARTIES IN WESTERN EUROPE.

Dean Acheson, US Secretary of State.

SOURCE

B

I BELIEVE THAT IT MUST BE THE POLICY OF THE UNITED STATES TO SUPPORT FREE PEOPLES WHO ARE RESISTING ATTEMPTED SUBJUGATION [control] BY ARMED MINORITIES OR OUTSIDE PRESSURES . . . THE FREE PEOPLES OF THE WORLD LOOK TO US FOR SUPPORT IN MAINTAINING THOSE FREEDOMS.

The Truman Doctrine, March 1947.

SOURCE

The events of 1947 had a lasting effect both upon East-West relations and upon Europe. In January 1947 the British and Americans merged their zones for greater economic efficiency. However, the superpowers were still talking to each other and the USSR was demobilising its troops. Why did the situation worsen?

The Truman Doctrine

In March 1947 the British, who had been supporting the monarchist government in Greece against communist rebels, announced their intention to withdraw and appealed to America for assistance. We know now that Stalin had kept his side of the agreement known as the 'percentages deal' which he made with Churchill in October 1944. By that agreement Romania and Bulgaria had been allocated to the Soviet Union's sphere of influence and Greece had been allocated to that of Great Britain. In 1947, however, US leaders assumed that the USSR was behind the flow of arms from Yugoslavia and Albania to help the Greek rebels and feared that if they did not intervene, communism would spread like a disease (source A).

When he made his speech to Congress on 12 March 1947 (source B), Truman had to convince both Congress and the American people of the need to spend vast sums of money on faraway countries, hence the strongly worded appeal in defence of democracy and 'free people' everywhere which became known as the **Truman Doctrine**.

In effect Truman offered US assistance to any country in the future which felt it was in danger from a communist threat. It was a huge undertaking, showing a commitment to oppose communism on a global scale and was in stark

*A British cartoon from **Punch** in October 1947.*

contrast to the isolationism of the inter-war years, when America had refused to involve itself in the world's problems. This was how the policy of containment would be carried out for decades. Thanks to the **Truman Doctrine** the Cold War extended beyond Europe, but Europe itself was the initial focus of attention.

Marshall Aid

The main fear of American leaders was not of a Soviet invasion of Western Europe but of the growth of communism in countries crippled by

13

D

A West German view of the Marshall Plan.

severe post-war economic problems. Consequently America made Europe's economic recovery its priority in 1947 for a number of reasons:
• The better off they were, the less likely it was that Europeans would turn to communism.
• They would need less American military aid or dollars.
• They could afford to buy American goods and this would be good for the US economy.

The Truman Doctrine justified US expenditure on Europe because that expenditure would be used to contain the spread of communism. As Truman said, the **Marshall Plan** and the Truman Doctrine were "two halves of the same walnut".

The severe winter of 1946-7 and the droughts of 1946 and 1947 had disrupted harvests, production and transport. The countries of western Europe had huge debts which they were unable to pay. The new Secretary of State, **George Marshall** returned from Europe in April and summarised the situation: "The patient is sinking while the doctors deliberate." In June 1947 Marshall proposed an **Economic Recovery Programme (ERP)** which would supply over 13 billion dollars to sixteen European countries between 1948 and 1952. He said: "Our policy is directed against hunger, poverty, desperation and chaos." Though the Americans were not keen to include the Soviet bloc in the Marshall Plan, they did not want it labelled as anti-Soviet either. Consequently **Marshall Aid** was offered to all European countries including the Soviet Union but only on condition that their economic records were available for scrutiny and their markets were open to Western goods. Not surprisingly Stalin refused such terms and put pressure on Eastern Europe to do the same. Stalin feared that Marshall Aid would lead to Germany's recovery and to Europe's dependence upon the USA. However the main problem was that the Soviets regarded Marshall Aid as a way of using American dollars to unite Europe against them and that even members of the Eastern bloc might be tempted by the US offer. Indeed both Poland and Czechoslovakia showed interest but the USSR prevented them joining the ERP.

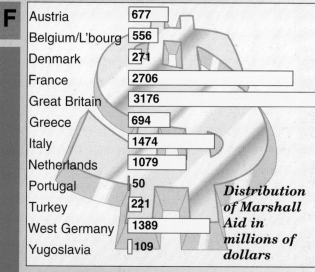

F		
Austria	677	
Belgium/L'bourg	556	
Denmark	271	
France	2706	
Great Britain	3176	
Greece	694	
Italy	1474	
Netherlands	1079	
Portugal	50	
Turkey	221	
West Germany	1389	
Yugoslavia	109	

Distribution of Marshall Aid in millions of dollars

SOURCE

A Soviet view of Marshall Aid.

Results of Marshall Aid

1 By 1952 Western Europe's industrial production was 35% higher than in 1939.

2 Marshall Aid revived European economies, increased world trade, and helped the post-war boom in America.

3 It deepened divisions not only between the superpowers but between Eastern and Western Europe. As the latter prospered, the differences in living standards on each side of the Iron Curtain became clearer.

4 Fear that their control of Eastern Europe might be undermined by the temptation of Marshall Aid caused the Soviets to tighten their grip. A communist government was set up in Hungary and in September 1947 the **Communist Information Bureau** (**Cominform**) was established. Its aim was to strengthen Soviet control over Eastern bloc countries.

5 In **February 1948** a communist coup in **Czechoslovakia** shocked the world. The Czechs distrusted the West which had deserted them in 1938 and were inclined to favour the Soviet Union. There was a strong communist party but **President Benes** had retained some non-communist members in the government. Now, under pressure from Soviet troops, an all-communist government was installed. The USA saw this as a clear demonstration of Soviet tactics and ambitions and there was a marked increase in support for Truman's containment policy. Two months after the Czech coup Congress accepted the Marshall Plan and, by implication, America's involvement in Europe's affairs.

6 In **January 1949** the USSR set up the **Council for Mutual Economic Assistance** (better known as **Comecon**). It was the Soviet Union's answer to the Marshall Plan and was intended to establish closer links between the USSR and Eastern Europe. As a result of **Comecon** Soviet trade with Eastern bloc countries had quadrupled by 1950.

?

1 What is the connection between sources A and B?

2 How did Marshall Aid support the policy of containment?

3 Using source E, explain why the Marshall Plan was so popular in America.

4 (a) Explain the Soviet view of Marshall Aid in source G. Why does this differ from source C?
(b) How did Marshall Aid affect Soviet policy in Eastern Europe?

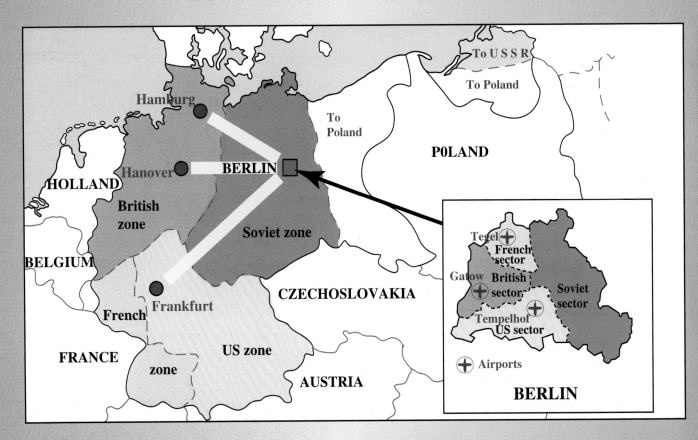

In 1947 the growing hostility between the Soviet Union in the east and the United States in the west was first described as **Cold War**. Over the next forty years this would be characterised by periods of tension and crisis alternating with periods of relative co-operation. However the crises were never allowed to escalate into all-out war as that would destroy both superpowers.

The first major crisis concerned Germany. Both sides recognised that Germany could play a crucial role in the centre of Europe, but the former Allies could not agree on what its future should be. America wanted German economic recovery to boost world trade, so it gave **Marshall Aid** to the western zones. The Soviet Union was concerned about its own recovery and wanted to keep Germany permanently weak to prevent yet another invasion.

In January 1948 the French zone was merged with the Anglo-American zone creating a single Western bloc. In June 1948 they introduced a new currency in their zone. Stalin, who was already alarmed by the increasing prosperity of the Western zones due to Marshall Aid, now decided on a trial of strength. He cut off Western access to Berlin. On the morning of 24 June Berliners woke to find that all roads, railways and canals leading to West Berlin had been closed due to technical difficulties!

The Berlin Blockade

Berlin lay 110 miles inside the Soviet zone. Though it was also divided into four zones and was therefore guarded by Western troops, the latter were too few in number and, since the West had no legal right of access, much depended upon Soviet goodwill to allow the free passage of goods overland between West Germany and West Berlin. The decision to blockade West Berlin on 24 June 1948 was Stalin's attempt to claw back control of events. The new currency would benefit West Berlin and highlight the economic differences between East and West, causing discontent in East Germany. By forcing the Allies out of Berlin, it would then become dependent upon the USSR. It would seem that Stalin gambled that the West would be reluctant to take action for fear of a war. There were over two million people in West Berlin and when the blockade was imposed they had only enough food for a month and coal for just ten days. Electricity supplies were also cut.

The Berlin Airlift

The US believed that if it did nothing to oppose the blockade, its whole position in Europe would collapse. As the American Commander, General Lucius Clay, said:

"When Berlin falls, Western Germany will be next. If we withdraw our position in Berlin,

Europe is threatened ... . Communism will run rampant."

West Berlin became a symbol of freedom which had to be upheld. The Americans dared not force their way through the road blocks as this could be viewed as an act of war. Consequently they decided to bring in supplies by air. Amid widespread scepticism they prepared for the biggest air operation in history. There were three airfields in West Berlin (the French hurriedly finished theirs) and each was in constant use, with planes landing on average every two minutes. One Berliner described the flow of silver grey planes as "a string of pearls in the sky," bringing hope as well as daily necessities. The massive airlift lasted 324 days with up to 13,000 tons delivered daily. Coal was a major import, but the planes carried everything from food, medicine and machinery to ping-pong balls and a guide dog! One pilot made tiny parachutes from handkerchiefs and dropped sweets for the children.

As the weather conditions deteriorated in the winter of 1948, the airlift became more dangerous. Ice, fog and collisions caused 79 casualties among the US and British pilots and German ground crews. However, though the Soviet planes deliberately flew close to the Allied planes, none were shot down, as that would have been seen as an act of war. During the blockade Berliners had to accept rationing, share fires and work by candlelight. Fortunately that winter was not severe. Despite the hardships, only a few were tempted by the offer of extra rations in the Russian sector. The determination of the Allies forced Stalin to lift the blockade on 12 May 1949.

A *British cartoon from 1948, called* **The Bird Watcher**. *The man with the gun is Stalin.*

Results

1 The Berlin Airlift was a huge propaganda defeat for the Soviets and a great boost for the West.
2 The confrontation in Germany encouraged Western countries to set up the **North Atlantic Treaty Organisation (NATO)** in April 1949. The common defence of Europe was based

Children watch from a fence as a US Airforce plane lands at Tempelhof Airport during the Berlin airlift.

17

on America's possession of the atomic bomb. As NATO's first Secretary-General, **Lord Ismay** said, it was designed "to keep the Americans in, the Germans down and the Russians out". His words are an important reminder that, although the Soviet threat was very important, the European powers still feared Germany and wanted to make sure the US remained in Europe.

3 The blockade made it clear that Germany could not be united and speeded up the process whereby it was divided into two separate states with different systems of government. In May 1949 the **German Federal Republic – West Germany** – was set up with its capital in Bonn, to be followed in October 1949 by the **German Democratic Republic – East Germany**. By the end of 1949 Churchill's prophecy of an 'iron curtain' had become reality.

4 The end of the blockade did not solve the problem of Berlin. It remained a flashpoint in East-West relations.

The crisis highlighted the dangers of superpower conflict by demonstrating the lengths to which both sides would go, short of all-out war. Just as importantly, it also showed the limitations each imposed. For instance, the Soviets did not use their larger army to force the West out of Berlin and the US did not use their atomic bomb. (Though they did move 60 B-29 bombers to Britain during the crisis. These planes could carry nuclear bombs.)

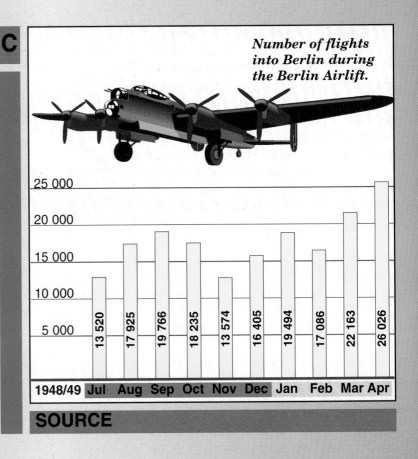

C

Number of flights into Berlin during the Berlin Airlift.

1948/49	Jul	Aug	Sep	Oct	Nov	Dec	Jan	Feb	Mar	Apr
	13 520	17 925	19 766	18 235	13 574	16 405	19 494	17 086	22 163	26 026

SOURCE

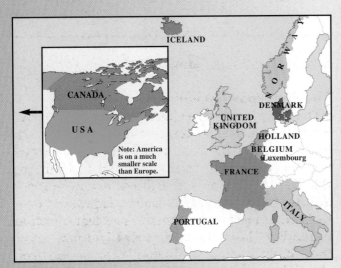

The original members of NATO in 1949.

?

1 Why did Stalin want the Allies to leave West Berlin and why were they so determined to stay?

2 "Neither superpower wanted war in 1948." Do you agree? Give reasons for your answer.

3 Make a timeline of the main events between 1945 and 1949.

4 Summarise the results of the Berlin Blockade in a web diagram.

1.6 THE KOREAN WAR 1950-53

Truman's increased popularity, following the success of the Berlin Airlift, was short lived. In August 1949 the USSR exploded an atomic bomb, thereby ending the US monopoly of nuclear weapons. On **1 October 1949** the **People's Republic of China** was proclaimed by **Mao Zedong**, leader of the victorious communist party, which had been engaged in bloody civil war with Chiang Kai-shek's Nationalist Party (KMT) since 1945. The US government had not expected the communist revolution in China to be successful. It had been supplying aid to the KMT for years, first to fight the Japanese (who had attacked China in 1937) and, more recently, to fight the communists.

The 'loss' of China to communism led to severe criticism of the US government's handling of foreign policy and brought fame to a junior senator from Wisconsin, **Joseph McCarthy**. The publicity surrounding the McCarthy 'witch-hunts' of suspected communists in public life created such a wave of anti-communism in America that, when the Korean war broke out, Truman had to act decisively to prove he was still tough on communism.

War breaks out

On the 25 June 1950 North Korean troops launched a surprise attack on South Korea. Within hours they had crossed the 38th Parallel, the line of latitude which, since 1945, had been the temporary border between the two states. Korea had formerly been under Japanese rule and, when Japan surrendered in August 1945, Soviet troops occupied the northern half of the peninsula, while American troops occupied the south. As in Germany, the superpowers failed to agree on how Korea would be reunited. Both supported different governments, neither of which acquired power through free elections. By 1948 North Korea had a communist government under **Kim Il-sung** and South Korea was governed by a dictator, **Syngman Rhee**. Both states had the same aim, which was to reunite the country, and this was the motive for the

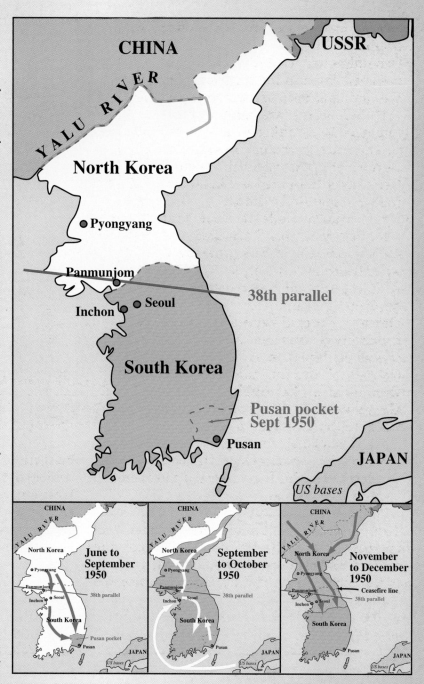

attack upon South Korea in 1950.

The Superpowers and Korea

The Americans were alarmed by the invasion of South Korea. Though a recent US defence review had suggested that the defence of South Korea was not of vital importance, Truman decided that the Soviet Union was behind North Korea's attack. Such an act of aggression had to be resisted, otherwise the whole American position in the Far East might be at risk. We now know that Stalin had only reluctantly supported Kim Il-sung's actions in order to stop North Korea becoming a Chinese satellite. Stalin was already worried that Mao, like Tito, would threaten the Soviet claim to be leader of the communist world. He was so anxious to avoid involvement in the conflict that, one week after the war began, he withdrew all Soviet pilots and advisers from North Korea. (In 1951 he did commit some aircraft to the defence of the Yalu river crossings, but they carried Chinese colours and the pilots wore Chinese uniforms.)

Truman's response to the invasion was immediate and decisive. He took the issue to the United Nations where the Security Council condemned the attack and ordered the use of armed intervention on behalf of South Korea. This was the only time between 1945 and 1990 that the UN agreed to use armed force against aggression and it was made possible by the fact that the USSR was temporarily boycotting the UN in protest against the refusal to admit the new People's Republic of China to the Security Council. The boycott meant the Soviet Union could not use its veto to block intervention. Truman appointed **General Douglas MacArthur** as Commander of the UN forces in Korea. Sixteen nations were nominally involved but the USA supplied 50% of the troops, 86% of the naval forces and 93% of the air power, and MacArthur took his orders from Truman, not from UN officials.

A smoking howitzer raises a cloud of dust as a US artillery crew blasts enemy positions on Korea's south-western front.

Containment or rollback?

The initial advance by the North Koreans took them deep into South Korea and by September only **Pusan** lay beyond their reach. MacArthur landed a force to their rear at **Inchon** and within a month had forced the North Koreans to retreat north of the 38th Parallel. At this point the aim of the original UN resolution had been achieved but, encouraged by success, Truman allowed MacArthur to cross the 38th Parallel to try to reunite the country. Ignoring Chinese warnings that they would be forced to intervene if their security was threatened by the US advance, MacArthur had pushed north to the **Yalu** river by the end of October.

Just as the Americans had underestimated the popularity of Mao's communist party before 1949, so they now underestimated China's anxiety as they drew closer to its border. In November 1950, 250,000 Chinese troops crossed that border and forced the UN troops to retreat south of the 38th Parallel once more. The Chinese troops were called 'volunteers' to avoid a formal declaration of war, which would likely have deepened the conflict.

Though MacArthur urged air strikes against China, and the American government debated the use of the atomic bomb, both ideas were rejected, as Washington feared that such action would lead to the Soviet Union's involvement. Truman abandoned the aim of all-out victory, which MacArthur wanted, in favour of a limited war in Korea and containment.

MacArthur was dismissed in April 1951 and returned to a hero's welcome. The war dragged on for a further two years with heavy losses on both sides, as each tried to gain a military advantage, and public dissatisfaction with the conduct of the war contributed to Truman's election defeat in 1952. An armistice was finally concluded in July 1953, despite Syngman Rhee's opposition, and a dispute over the exchange of

A US army helicopter delivers a sling of heavy timber to the troops building a defence line in Korea.

?

1 Why did America intervene in the Korean War?

2 How successful was US intervention in Korea? Complete a table as shown below:

Successful	Not successful

3 What were the long term effect of the Korean War?

prisoners of war, because two-thirds of the Chinese POWs refused to return home.

The consequences of the Korean War

'The century's nastiest little war' was a milestone in the Cold War and in East-West relations. It established a pattern whereby if one superpower was directly involved, the other took care to be only indirectly associated. Its effects were both long lasting and far reaching.

1 There were over two million killed in a war which largely confirmed the status quo, as it existed in June 1950. The border remained near to the 38th Parallel; the peninsula remained divided. There was no peace treaty, though the agreement of 1953 proved surprisingly durable, despite the bitterness and tension between the two countries.

2 Truman and the Democrats were defeated in the elections of 1952, thus ending what McCarthy described as 'twenty years of treason'.

3 The war confirmed America's commitment to containment on a global scale. Not only did it continue to support South Korea but also **Taiwan**, the last stronghold of Chiang Kai-shek. Thanks to US military and economic aid, Taiwan survived as an independent state and continued to hold China's seat on the Security Council.

4 The US role in the Korean war, together with US support for Chiang Kai-shek, embittered relations with China for almost twenty years. *"700 million potential customers had turned into the apparition of 700 million dangerous adversaries."*
(AT Steele, quoted by W Lafeber.)

5 To counter the perceived communist threat in Asia, the US signed a treaty with the Philippines in August 1951 and another with Australia and New Zealand in September 1951 (the **ANZUS Pact**). Both committed the US to defence of the area. Korea also influenced the decision to send American personnel to South Vietnam.

6 The most dramatic change occurred in relations with Japan. The Korean war hastened the end of the US occupation of Japan and a peace treaty was signed in September 1951. Japan was now of vital importance to US policy in Asia, so the Americans helped rebuild the Japanese economy, so that Japan would not be vulnerable to communism.

7 The war turned NATO into a full-blown military alliance. Truman tripled defence expenditure, so that America could meet the Soviet threat anywhere in the world. The number of US troops in Europe was increased and the way prepared for the rearmament of West Germany. With the explosion of the hydrogen bomb by both America and the Soviet Union by 1953, the arms race was well and truly under way.

*A cartoon showing the Soviet attitude to the Western allies admitting West Germany to NATO in 1955. Britain says to France "Don't worry, he's on a chain." The links of the chain are paper and each says **security** in Russian. The dog is chained to a $ sign.*

B

YOU HAVE A ROW OF DOMINOES SET UP. YOU KNOCK OVER THE FIRST ONE. WHAT WILL HAPPEN TO THE LAST ONE IS THE CERTAINTY THAT IT WILL GO OVER VERY QUICKLY. ASIA HAS ALREADY LOST SOME 450 MILLIONS OF ITS PEOPLES TO COMMUNIST DICTATORSHIP. WE SIMPLY CAN'T AFFORD GREATER LOSSES.

President Eisenhower, April 1954.

SOURCE

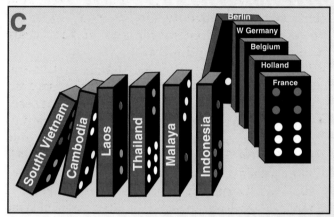

The 'domino theory' 1954

The public statements of American leaders contributed to the Soviet obsession with security. **President Dwight Eisenhower (1953-60)** had to please a Republican Congress which wanted an aggressive (but cheap) foreign policy, and his Secretary of State, John Foster Dulles, was noted as much for his forthright comments as for his anti-Soviet views,*"To all those suffering under Communist slavery, let us say: 'You can count on us'*. Both men spoke of 'rolling back' communism and of liberating the people of Eastern Europe. Further evidence of this tough stance was 'the domino theory' which Eisenhower explained in April 1954 (sources B and C).

Like Truman, Eisenhower supported the containment of communism which was why the USA was pouring money into French Indochina (Vietnam) but, after their recent experiences in Korea, the Americans refused the French request for troops in 1954. They preferred instead to develop a network of alliances — hence the creation of SEATO (South East Asia Treaty Organisation) in 1954 to defend the Far East and the Baghdad Pact of 1955 which aimed to defend the Middle East.

Since 1950 America had supported West German rearmament and membership of **NATO**, but the French and the Soviets opposed the idea. They recalled how German armies had invaded their countries in both world wars and feared that rearmament, combined with economic recovery, would make Germany a threat once more. Only when America promised to keep troops in Europe did the French abandon their objections to the proposal and **West Germany** was finally **admitted to NATO in May 1955**.

Despite its name, NATO membership already extended to Italy, Greece and Turkey, the latter providing military bases which, from a Soviet point of view, were rather too close for comfort. Now West German rearmament, as a consequence of NATO membership, increased the threat to Soviet security and led to the formation of the **Warsaw Pact** later in May. The Pact was a military alliance of all the communist countries of Eastern Europe, with the exception of Yugoslavia, and they undertook to defend each other, if one was attacked.

Khrushchev and 'peaceful co-existence'

The death of Stalin in March 1953 had prompted speculation about a possible thaw in the Cold War. This was because the West had perceived Stalin as their main opponent, the individual responsible for the deepening distrust and hostility which had dominated East-West relations since 1945. Eisenhower voiced his hopes for change:

"The new Soviet leadership has a precious opportunity to help turn the tide of history... We welcome every act of peace."

By 1955 **Nikita Khrushchev** had emerged as the new Soviet leader. His genial personality contrasted favourably with the brooding presence of his predecessor and at first there were grounds for optimism:

- The post-war occupation of Austria by the four Allied powers ended in 1954 and Austrian independence and neutrality were guaranteed.
- In July 1955 at the Geneva summit conference the leaders of America and the Soviet Union met for the first time since Potsdam in 1945. They reached no agreement on major issues such as Germany, but the summit created goodwill and encouraged further meetings, as at Camp David, near Washington in 1959.
- **Cominform**, the organisation set up by Stalin to ensure that the Eastern bloc countries followed instructions from Moscow, was dissolved.
- In February 1956 Khrushchev made his famous speech denouncing Stalin's policies and urging 'peaceful co-existence' with the West. The call for peaceful co-existence was inspired by fear of a nuclear war, which forced both superpowers to find ways of resolving difficulties without fighting each other. The USSR would continue to support communist revolutions elsewhere in the world but through peaceful means, and Khrushchev acknowledged that there were "different roads to Socialism". The speech was of major importance in shaping Soviet foreign policy. However its immediate impact was most strongly felt within the Soviet satellite states of Eastern Europe. The harsh criticism of Stalin, the architect of post-war Eastern Europe, implied that his policies there were also wrong and could now be reversed. Ironically, the speech which seemed the most positive sign so far of a thaw in East-West relations was the direct cause of events which, by the end of 1956, revealed how little had really changed.

Reaction

Khrushchev's speech of February 1956 seemed to offer the prospect of greater freedom within the Eastern bloc. The satellite countries had to provide the USSR with reparations in food and goods, while their own standard of living fell and their people lived in fear of secret police and labour camps. Now the resentment surfaced, first in Poland and then in Hungary.

In July 1956 the Poles rebelled against the high food prices and low wages. Fifty three workers were killed in riots. Having sent Soviet tanks into Warsaw to restore order, Khrushchev then visited Poland where he agreed to some reforms and, most importantly, accepted **Gomulka**, a popular and moderate communist, as the new leader.

The Hungarian Uprising, 1956

The unrest in Poland spread to Hungary where there were also demands for reform. On 23 October students took to the streets and were supported by the workers and the Hungarian army. As the riots spread another popular communist leader, **Imre Nagy** was brought back to power. On 28 October Soviet tanks began to withdraw and, confident of American support, pressure mounted for various reforms.

On 1 November Imre Nagy announced the decision to introduce free elections and to leave the Warsaw Pact. The Soviets could not allow their satellite to overthrow its communist

A Soviet tank on the streets of Budapest, 1956.

government and leave the Warsaw Pact, because such action would destroy the unity of the Soviet bloc and weaken the USSR's defences.

On **4 November 1956**, 6000 Soviet tanks crossed the Hungarian border and, in the bitter street fighting which followed, 30,000 were killed. Imre Nagy sought refuge in the Yugoslav embassy but was captured and later executed. Appeals for aid were all in vain. In the midst of the uprising the attention of the West was on the Anglo-French invasion of Suez, which became America's main concern. Eisenhower was also campaigning for re-election. Besides, there was the problem of actually getting to Hungary. Austria was neutral and NATO forces could not advance through it. Khrushchev also threatened Britain and France with rockets if they attempted to interfere.

Results of the Hungarian Uprising

- Hungary was placed under strict communist control.
- It gave a clear warning to the Soviet Union's other satellites and none dared try for greater independence for another twenty years.
- Khrushchev's call for peaceful co-existence now had a hollow ring. Clearly Soviet control of its satellites would not weaken, nor would anti-Communist views be tolerated within the Eastern bloc.
- Khrushchev was criticised at home for his handling of the affair and needed a foreign policy success to re-establish his position.
- Eisenhower also faced criticism. The Truman Doctrine and recent talk about 'roll-back' suggested Eisenhower would help the Hungarians, but he did nothing. He realised it was too dangerous to challenge the USSR in Eastern Europe. So, despite the tough talk, in reality the USA accepted that Eastern Europe was a Soviet sphere of influence.

The Berlin crisis 1958

Since 1949 money was poured into West Berlin to turn it into a showpiece for capitalism and highlight the comparative poverty of East Germany. East Germans could travel freely into West Berlin and, if they wished, they need never return home. Berlin was a hole in the Iron Curtain. Over two million East Germans escaped to the West between 1949 and 1958. The refugees, or defectors, were usually young educated people whose defection was a loss to the economy of East Germany. West Berlin was also ideally situated for spreading anti-Soviet propaganda and for spying on East Germany.

The USSR wanted Western recognition of East Germany as an independent state and, in 1958, Khrushchev engineered a crisis to force the West to agree. He gave them an ultimatum. They had six months in which to negotiate a peace treaty with Germany and leave Berlin, which would become a 'free city'. If they failed to do so then

---

E THE HUNGARIAN REBELS WOULD FIRE ON THE TANKS FROM UPPER STOREY WINDOWS, THEN AS THE MIGHTY T-34S RUMBLED UP, THEIR GREAT GUNS RAISED, A SMALL BOY WOULD LEAP OUT OF A DOORWAY, FLING A PAIL OF PETROL OVER THE TANK'S ENGINE COMPARTMENT AND LEAP BACK TO SHELTER. AS THE TANK TOOK FIRE AND ITS CREW SCRAMBLED OUT OF THE TURRET, THE YOUNG TOMMY-GUNNER FIRING FROM THE WINDOWS WOULD MOW THEM DOWN. ANOTHER WAY WAS TO SLOSH A BUCKET OF PETROL ACROSS A STREET AND THROW A MATCH IN IT JUST AS A SOVIET TANK PLUNGED PAST.

Extract from Time *magazine, 12 November 1956*

SOURCE

F THE WESTERN POWERS IN BERLIN USE IT AS A CENTRE OF SUBVERSIVE [UNDERHAND] ACTIVITY AGAINST THE GDR. IN NO OTHER PART OF THE WORLD ARE SO MANY ESPIONAGE CENTRES TO BE FOUND. THESE CENTRES SMUGGLE THEIR AGENTS INTO THE GDR FOR ALL KINDS OF SUBVERSION: RECRUITING SPIES; SABOTAGE; PROVOKING DISTURBANCES.
THE GOVERNMENT PRESENTS ALL WORKING PEOPLE OF THE GDR WITH A PROPOSAL THAT WILL SECURELY BLOCK SUBVERSIVE ACTIVITY SO THAT RELIABLE SAFEGUARDS AND EFFECTIVE CONTROL WILL BE ESTABLISHED AROUND WEST BERLIN, INCLUDING ITS BORDER WITH DEMOCRATIC BERLIN.
A Soviet explanation for the building of the Berlin Wall, 1961.

SOURCE

G

An East German refugee crawls through a tunnel under the Berlin Wall in October 1964. Fifty seven people escaped before the tunnel was discovered. East German guards poured gunfire through it before sealing it.

along the border between East and West Berlin, stopping all movement between the sectors. Overnight people lost their jobs and families were separated. The wire was quickly replaced by a concrete wall which became a symbol of communist oppression and the most visible reminder of the Iron Curtain. Despite the guards on the wall to prevent defectors crossing to the West, many East Germans still tried to escape and often died in the attempt (source G). Khrushchev withdrew his threat to make a separate peace treaty with East Germany, but his latest failure to drive the West out of Berlin further increased his need for a success abroad.

The change of leadership in the USSR did not, therefore, fulfil expectations of a thaw in East-West relations, because the issues which had originally divided the superpowers remained unchanged, and the leaders of each had to be seen to serve his country's best interests. Consequently Eisenhower and Dulles sounded aggressive though they proved cautious in crises, while Khrushchev sounded conciliatory until Soviet security or his own political power came under threat.

the USSR would sign a separate treaty with East Germany which would have control of all access to Berlin. Since the West was anxious to avoid another crisis like the Berlin blockade almost as much as they wanted to avoid war, the ultimatum was a serious threat. Dean Rusk, the US Secretary of State commented, "When I go to sleep at night I try not to think about Berlin."

The West refused to be drawn and Khrushchev backed down. His visit to the USA in 1959 was generally successful in easing tensions but, increasingly, China criticised him for giving in to the West. He needed to improve his personal prestige so he renewed his threat to Berlin in June 1961.

The Berlin Wall

Khrushchev may have hoped that the newly elected American President — **John F Kennedy** — so recently embarrassed by the Bay of Pigs incident (see Ch 1.9) would be easier to bluff. However Kennedy stood firm in defence of West Berlin, and Khrushchev was forced to find a solution to the refugee problem.

On the morning of **13 August 1961** East German soldiers erected a barbed wire fence

?

1 What point was the cartoonist making in source A?

2 (a) Summarise the ways in which the US supported the policy of containment during the 1950s.
   (b) Why did it fail to do so in Hungary in 1956?

3 How did events in Hungary and Berlin demonstrate the Soviet obsession with security?

4 How reliable is source F as an explanation for the building of the Berlin Wall?

1.8 The Arms Race 1945-1962

The relationship between the superpowers was further complicated by the nuclear arms race and their perceptions of each other's strength and motives. The explosion of the **Soviet Union's first atomic bomb** in **1949** started the arms race. Since 1945 the USA had had a monopoly of nuclear weapons but with the surprising revelation that the USSR had caught up so quickly, the race was on to build a bigger, more powerful bomb - the **hydrogen bomb** whose power was nearly 1,000 times greater than that of the atomic bomb which destroyed Hiroshima in 1945. The Americans made their first successful test in 1952, followed

A British view of the arms race, 1960. America and Russia are in the lead, followed by Britain and France.

soon after by the Russians in 1953. Since both superpowers now possessed nuclear weapons capable of destruction on a massive scale, both had to consider the circumstances in which such weapons could and should be used.

During the Cold War both superpowers threatened to use nuclear weapons as a means of pressure. For instance, the Americans threatened China during the Korean War, while Khrushchev made similar threats over Suez in 1956 and Berlin in 1961. Threats were also useful as a means of convincing each other of the will to use nuclear bombs. However, both recognised the dangers involved since they risked reprisal. Consequently, Eisenhower refused to use nuclear weapons to help US allies in the Far East, while Khrushchev backed down in the Cuban Missile Crisis. He predicted at the time that in a nuclear war "the survivors would envy the dead".

Despite the realisation that a nuclear war could bring mutual destruction, both superpowers continued to develop nuclear weapons, even while reaching agreement on safeguards and limitations. In the 1960s the Soviet Union built a bomb with the force of 57,000,000 tons of TNT. The first atomic bombs only had the force of 15,000 tons of TNT.

Why was there an arms race?

Though both superpowers were reluctant to actually use nuclear weapons, each feared its opponent would gain a military advantage. If some balance of nuclear strength could be achieved, the realisation that each had the power to destroy its opponent would **deter** any nuclear attack or **first strike**. Therefore the possession of nuclear weapons was seen as a means of defence.

The Eisenhower administration relied more upon the **nuclear deterrent** because the Republican Congress wanted to reduce government expenditure. As one Presidential aide commented, nuclear weapons were cheaper than conventional armed forces and offered "a bigger bang for the buck". As a result the US nuclear stockpile doubled between 1953 and 1955. Eisenhower was the first US President to treat atomic weapons as 'conventional' (ie like tanks, infantry, etc). In 1955 he stated publicly that they were "to be used exactly as you would use a bullet or anything else".

The US policy of **massive retaliation** depended upon the nuclear deterrent. This meant that if the USSR attacked NATO forces in Europe, the USA would use nuclear weapons in retaliation to destroy Russian cities, rather than front-line troops. The policy created a tough image and gave the impression that the USA would actually use nuclear weapons. As a result the USSR, whose territory could be directly threatened by NATO, expanded its nuclear arsenal, at the same time as Khrushchev was urging peaceful co-existence.

In 1957 Americans were shocked by the launch

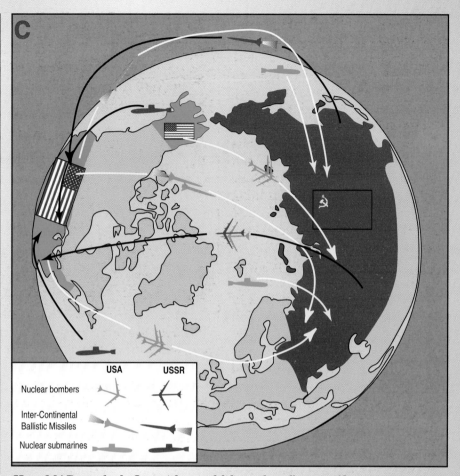

*How MAD worked. One side would launch a **first strike** against enemy missile sites. Using mobile missile launchers the other side could immediately retaliate with those missiles which were still intact. The scale of the attacks means both sides are devastated.*

Legend:
USA / USSR
- Nuclear bombers
- Inter-Continental Ballistic Missiles
- Nuclear submarines

SOURCE B

of the first **Russian Sputnik** into space. It was not the Sputnik or satellite which they feared, but the rocket which launched it, for this rocket could be fitted with a nuclear warhead which could be fired at a target thousands of miles away. This technological development had major implications for the arms race.

1 Both sides increased military expenditure as they rushed to build **ICBMs** (**Inter-continental ballistic missiles**), which had a range of 1500 to 8000 miles.

2 For the first time American cities and civilians could be attacked. America's own security was now under threat for no country was safe from long range missiles.

3 If the nuclear deterrent was to work, then the USA had to develop **second strike capability** so that, even when attacked, the country could still respond and launch missiles which would destroy the attacker. Therefore nuclear weapons had to be protected from a first strike either by being located underground or on **mobile missile launchers**, such as planes and submarines. This led, in 1960, to the development of Polaris submarines, which carried nuclear warheads with a range of 1500 miles.

4 **Second strike capability** was the basis of **Mutual Assured Destruction** (**MAD**). Since neither superpower could destroy all its rival's nuclear weapons in a single attack, neither could afford to attack first for fear of total destruction.

During the late 1950s, Americans thought the Soviets were ahead in the arms race. They estimated that the USSR would have 500 ICBMs by the end of 1960, and 1000 by the end of 1961 – compared to 30 American missiles in 1960 and 70 in 1961. In fact the Soviet Union had fewer than 50 ICBMs in 1961 and remained outnumbered. Thanks to spy plane flights over the USSR, the US government knew that the Soviet advantage was a myth, but Eisenhower did not make this public because he wanted to prevent a Soviet build-up in missiles. Not until the late 1960s did Russia finally achieve parity in nuclear weapons (see source F).

Date	Event	Country
Oct 1957	Sputnik launched	USSR
Nov 1957	A dog (Laika) was sent into space	USSR
Sept 1959	First rocket reached the moon	USSR
Oct 1959	First photographs of the dark side of the moon	USSR
April 1960	Weather satellite sent photographs back to earth	USA
April 1961	First man (Yuri Gagarin) to orbit earth (two hours)	USSR
Feb 1962	First American (John Glenn) to orbit earth	USA
June 1963	First woman (Valentina Terestikova) to orbit earth	USSR
Oct 1967	First spacecraft to land on another planet	USSR
1968	First satellite placed in orbit around the moon	USSR
Dec 1968	First men to orbit the moon	USA
21 July 1969	First man on the moon (Neil Armstrong)	USA

SOURCE

An early Russian space rocket.

The space race

The launch of the Sputnik had one other unforeseen and very costly result — the space race. Up until 1957 Americans had been confident of their technological superiority. The Sputnik was not only alarming evidence of Soviet expertise, but also a major Soviet success in the Cold War. Both countries now started on an expensive space programme designed to enhance their prestige, as well as improve their military strength. In 1959 America spent 150 million dollars on its space programme. By 1966 it was spending 5500 million dollars. The USSR was equally committed to a crippling expenditure on the arms and space race at a time when its productivity slowed and consumer goods remained scarce. The main developments in the space race are shown in source D.

The space race did have some beneficial results. Both sides found satellites helpful in policing the arms race, as they could take photographs of enemy missile bases. Peaceful uses included weather observation and improved communications. The most dramatic effects could be seen on television with 'live' pictures transmitted across the world. Events such as the Olympics, Armstrong on the moon in 1969, and the war in Vietnam, could be watched as they happened. The influence of television upon public opinion grew apace. Research for the space programme also produced **teflon** which is used for non-stick pans.

The 'Battle of the Conjurors'

Tight security surrounded developments in the nuclear arms race and the space race. Former Vice-President Harry Truman only learned of the **Manhattan Project** (for the development of the atomic bomb) after he became President. In view of the secrecy, the speed with which the Soviets produced their first atomic bomb in 1949 was suspicious and proved to be the result of spying. **Klaus Fuchs**, a German-born communist who had worked on the Manhattan Project, passed the relevant papers to the Soviets, enabling them to copy the American weapon.

The dangerous rivalry between the superpowers during the Cold War meant that each side used spies to find out what the other was doing, or thinking of doing, and act accordingly. Truman established the **CIA (Central Intelligence Agency)** in 1947 and Khrushchev formed the **KGB**. The extent of spying by both sides was unusual in peacetime and reflected the suspicion and hostility between them. Churchill described the world of spying as the 'battle of the conjurors', a contest which captured the public imagination, thanks to popular fiction and numerous Holywood films portraying the undercover world of spies — eg the James Bond film *To Russia with Love* and *The Spy who came in from the Cold*, which was based on a bestseller written by John le Carré. For once the storyline in the novels and films was no stranger than the real world of spying.

- Both sides used similar methods including **surveillance** and **covert operations**, where agents tried to overthrow unfriendly governments For instance, the CIA succeeded in overthrowing the government of **Guatemala** in **1954**, but failed in Cuba in the **Bay of Pigs** fiasco in **1961** (see Ch 1.9).
- Undercover agents were placed in government positions, where they had access to useful information. **Guy Burgess**, **Donald MacLean** and **Kim Philby** were all British diplomats and Soviet spies. They defected before they could be arrested.
- Double agents worked for both sides, though only one side knew! Such agents could supply false information to mislead the enemy.
- Sexual seduction and blackmail were used to make government officials betray their

country's secrets. William Vassall, a homosexual, was blackmailed with compromising photographs taken at a party in Moscow.

- Both sides imposed the death penalty upon spies who had betrayed their country. The Americans executed the Rosenbergs in 1953 and the Soviets executed Oleg Penkovsky, a KGB colonel, in 1963 for passing secrets to British businessman Greville Wynne.
- Both sides tried to protect their agents, whose

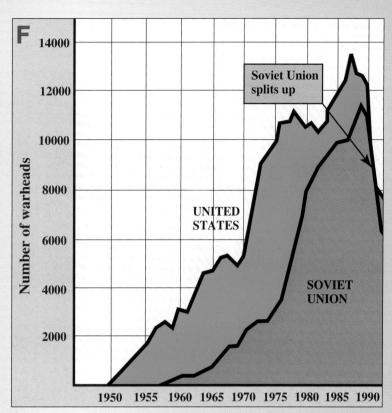

The Nuclear Arms Race 1949 to 1990.

The Glienicker Bridge in Berlin, where spies were exchanged between East and West during the Cold War.

*Poster for a James Bond movie **From Russia With Love**.*

secrets they could not afford to allow fall into enemy hands. Captured agents could be rescued, eg George Blake, who escaped from Wormwood Scrubs in 1966, or they might be exchanged for enemy agents of equal importance and value. For instance, **Gary Powers** was exchanged in 1962 for a KGB colonel, who had received a 30 year sentence in America in 1957.

- While satellites could provide useful information without risking a life, the USA also used the **U2 spy plane**. These planes could fly at high altitude to protect them from enemy fire. It was a U2 spy flight over the Soviet Union in 1960 which provoked a quarrel that destroyed the Paris summit.

The U2 incident, 1960

In May 1960 Gary Powers, a member of the CIA, took off from Pakistan to make a long distance flight over the USSR. The purpose of the mission was to take photographs of Soviet missile sites. Each flight, including this one, was authorised by President Eisenhower. The plane was shot down and Powers was captured. Khrushchev then announced that a plane had been shot down, but gave no details, which led the Americans to assume that Powers was dead. They released a statement admitting the loss of a research plane being used to study weather conditions and denied spying upon the Soviet Union. When Khrushchev then released the full details, the Americans were shown to have lied. Once the USA admitted to spying, Khrushchev demanded an apology. He agreed to meet Eisenhower at the Paris summit providing he admitted the flight took place without his permission. This Eisenhower refused to do since it would look as if he was not in control of his country's defence policy.

Eisenhower did promise that there would be no more spy flights, but refused to apologise and the Paris summit ended in uproar. The USSR condemned America's action at the UN and, amidst mounting tension, US forces were put on worldwide alert. While Eisenhower later admitted he had made a mistake in authorising the flight, Khrushchev's motives are less clear. One theory is that he wanted to please (and silence) his critics at home, and in China, by getting tougher with America.

It was another U2 mission, following the disastrous covert operation in the Bay of Pigs, which plunged the superpowers into their most dangerous confrontation of the Cold War — the **Cuban Missile Crisis**.

?

1 Which superpower was winning the arms race in the 1940s, 1950s and 1960s? How did this affect its rival?
Which was winning the space race between 1957 and 1968? How did this affect its rival?

2 Using the evidence in this unit explain why possession of nuclear weapons by both superpowers acted as a deterrent.

3 What are the strengths and weaknesses of source F as historical evidence?

4 How did spying contribute to dangerous tensions between the superpowers?

30

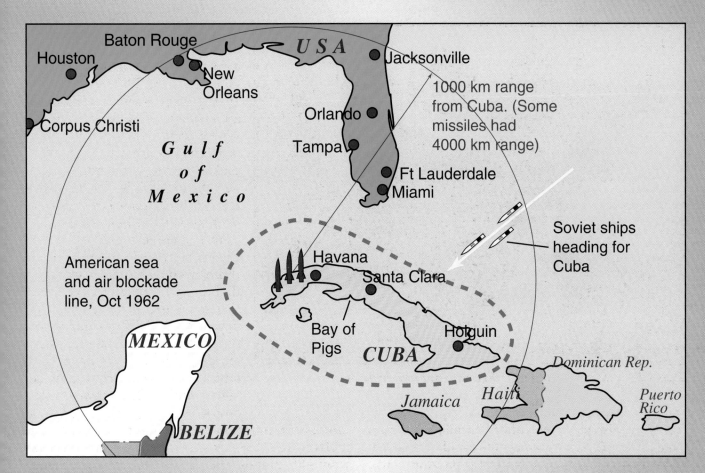

The origins of the Cuban Missile Crisis can be found in 1959, when **Fidel Castro**'s supporters finally overthrew Batista's military dictatorship, which had been in power since 1953. Within a year Castro had introduced reforms, such as nationalisation (state ownership) of various companies, and of land, which was redistributed to the peasants. He also brought communists into the government and relations with the USA steadily worsened.

Why did America oppose Castro?
1 Batista was a corrupt dictator, but he had been careful to stay friendly with America and, up until 1959, most of Cuba's trade in sugar and cigars was with America.
2 Though Castro was not officially known to be a communist in 1959, the Americans suspected this from the start. His policies, such as nationalisation, seemed to confirm their fears and what made it worse was the fact that some of the companies, and land, taken over by Castro's government, belonged to American citizens.
3 As a result Eisenhower refused to meet Castro, when he visited America in 1959, and he refused loans and economic aid. When Castro

turned to the USSR for help, the USA banned all trade with Cuba. Such tough tactics only made Cuba more dependent upon the Soviets. By 1962, 80% of Cuba's trade was with countries in the Soviet bloc, and Soviet arms and troops had also arrived.
4 As Castro drew closer to the USSR, American hostility hardened into determination to overthrow him. Castro now openly paraded his communist sympathies, and the American government would not tolerate a communist country within their sphere of influence. Cuba was only 90 miles from the American coast and America had consistently warned European countries against interference in the American continent. The countries of Central America, and the Caribbean especially, were seen as 'America's backyard'. In view of America's opposition to communism across the globe since 1945, the existence and proximity of a pro-Soviet communist government in Cuba was bound to endanger and annoy.

The Bay of Pigs, April 1961
Eisenhower approved a CIA covert operation against Castro before he left office, and Kennedy inherited the plan for an invasion force of 1500

CIA–trained Cuban exiles to land and encourage a general uprising to overthrow Castro. Kennedy made some important, and disastrous, changes to the original plan. The landing was now to take place in the Bay of Pigs, where there had been virtually no reconnaissance (photographs of coral reefs were mistaken for seaweed), and he refused to authorise a second US air strike, should it be requested.

The result, in April 1961, was a disaster which reflected badly upon the Americans, and Kennedy in particular, and boosted Castro's reputation in equal measure. In the Bay of Pigs some landing craft were wrecked by the coral reefs; the initial CIA air strike failed to destroy all the Cuban planes; contrary to intelligence reports the local population did not flock to support the invasion; those troops not killed in the assault were quickly rounded up by the 20,000 strong Cuban army.

After the Bay of Pigs fiasco Castro relied on the Soviets more than ever. US covert operations continued with propaganda, plans to assassinate Castro and raids which were carried out in 1962. In such circumstances it is not surprising that Castro agreed, in May 1962, to allow Soviet missiles to be stationed in Cuba.

John F Kennedy addressing a news conference during the Cuban crisis.

Nikita Khrushchev pictured on the cover of Time magazine, issue dated 22 July 1957.

Why did Khrushchev put missiles in Cuba?

Since America's protective attitude towards her own 'backyard' was well known, Khrushchev's reasons for placing missiles in Cuba remain puzzling. The Soviets' own insistence upon having friendly states on their borders caused them to crush the Hungarian Revolution in 1956, and both superpowers appeared to accept the unwritten rule of spheres of influence, which was why the Americans did nothing to help the Hungarians.

Khrushchev wrote in his memoirs in 1971 that he acted to protect Cuba (Source F)

However, an equally likely explanation is that he saw an opportunity to off set America's nuclear superiority and to equalise her strength, by placing cheaper short and medium range missiles in Cuba. This would have doubled the effectiveness of a Soviet nuclear attack upon the USA but at limited expense.

Other factors included:
- Khrushchev's need for a major success in foreign policy to strengthen his personal position in the Soviet Union and abroad.
- The Soviet leader had already tried bluff and threats over Berlin and showed a tendency to take risks.
- He thought Kennedy was a young and inexperienced opponent, whose weakness could be exploited.

The thirteen days

The first missiles arrived in Cuba in **September 1962**. Since the Soviet Union had always placed nuclear missile sites within her own borders, the American government was slow to realise the danger. It was French intelligence sources who alerted the new head of the CIA, who was on honeymoon in Paris. He demanded a U2 flight over Cuba and finally got one on **14 October**. The photographs provided clear evidence of the missile sites, which ended any hopes that Khrushchev had of fooling the Americans. The sites were not camouflaged in any way, because the Soviet technicians sent to do the job followed exactly the same procedures as they used at home, where camouflage was unnecessary. The clear evidence of missiles pointed at American cities and an estimated 80 million people shook the US government.

This view from the air shows part of a load of fifteen bombers and missiles aboard a Soviet ship, the Kasimov, *sailing off Cuba in 1962.*

16 October: Kennedy was informed. He then set up the **Executive Committee (Excomm)** to deal with the crisis. The **Excomm** met daily. They decided against negotiating with Moscow as it would be too slow. Kennedy did, however, use his brother, Bobby, as a contact with the Soviet ambassador in Washington.

17 October: Kennedy got Khrushchev's assurance that he had no intentions of installing missiles in Cuba.

20 October: Having decided against a full scale invasion, or an air strike, both of which would cause Soviet casualties and likely lead to war, Kennedy decided on a naval blockade around Cuba. This would prevent Soviet ships, known to be carrying missiles, from reaching Cuba. It also forced Khrushchev to make the next move.

22 October: Kennedy addressed the nation on television, announcing the discovery of the missile sites and his decision to impose a blockade. The news stunned the world.

23 October: A blockade zone around Cuba was established. Americans waited for the Soviet response.

24 October: To everyone's relief the Soviet ships stopped before reaching the blockade. Those thought to be carrying nuclear warheads turned back. However the missiles in Cuba still had to be removed and there was no guarantee that nuclear warheads had not got through already.

26 October: Kennedy received the first letter from Khrushchev in which he said he would remove the missiles, if Kennedy promised not to invade Cuba.

27 October: A second letter arrived. This took a tougher line and demanded that US missiles in Turkey be removed as well. To which letter should they respond? During the discussions news reached Washington that a U2 plane had been shot down over Cuba and the pilot killed. Tensions were high. Military commanders recommended an air strike on Monday, followed by invasion. Only the President continued o urge caution. His brother suggested a way out of the dilemma was to answer the first letter, as if the second had not been received. They accepted Khrushchev's offer but, through the Soviet ambassador, Kennedy issued a strong warning of the consequences if it was rejected. He also promised that the missiles in Turkey would be dismantled, but insisted that this would remain an informal and secret agreement.

28 October: Khrushchev accepted and the crisis was over.

An American cartoon of 1962.

A British cartoon of 1962.

How dangerous was the crisis?

People at the time were very worried. Many thought a nuclear war was imminent. U Thant, the Secretary-General of the UN, appealed to both sides to do all they could to avoid the disaster of nuclear war. One Soviet general said: *"The slightest spark or false move by either side could have triggered a nuclear catastrophe."*

It was a stark choice between co-existence and non-existence.

° Both superpowers were on full scale alert. The USA had over 50 bombers armed with nuclear warheads continuously in the air during the crisis. When one landed, another took off. In the event of a Soviet first strike, the bombers would have been able to deliver the US response. Nuclear missiles were also armed.

° Though Kennedy had to consider the possibility that nuclear warheads were already in Cuba, he appears to have thought that, on balance, they were not and made decisions accordingly. It is now known that there were 9 short, and 36 medium, range nuclear missiles all armed and ready in Cuba. When Robert McNamara, Defence Secretary and a member of the **Excomm** found this out in 1992, he was deeply shaken, knowing that they had been 24 hours away from launching an attack on the island.

° The CIA thought there were 12,000-16,000 Soviet troops in Cuba during the crisis. In fact there were 42,000 and, if Washington had known, this would have raised tensions even further.

° The shooting down of the U2 came at the most critical point of the crisis, on 27 October, while the **Excomm** debated their response to Khrushchev. Such an act could have plunged both sides into war. It is still uncertain whether it was a Cuban or Soviet action but the possibility that the local Soviet commander would have been left in control of nuclear missiles, if communications with Moscow broke down, was alarming for both superpowers.

How was the crisis defused?

Khrushchev made the mistake of challenging the Americans in the Caribbean, where their naval power proved decisive. Since he did not want a nuclear war, he had no alternative but to allow his ships to turn back.

Both sides acted with restraint in their efforts to avoid a nuclear war. The Americans did not react to the loss of the U2, nor did the Soviets react to the U2 flight over Siberia on the same day, nor to the US navy's action in forcing a Soviet submarine to the surface, near their blockade line. Both allowed their opponents to retreat without too much loss of face. Kennedy was careful not to boast of victory, and paid tribute to Khrushchev's 'contribution to peace', while Khrushchev did not reveal the concession Kennedy secretly made over the missiles in Turkey.

Results

1 Within months of the crisis the missiles in both Turkey and Cuba were dismantled. Castro was furious and refused to allow the UN inspectors into Cuba to confirm that the missiles really had been dismantled, with the result that Kennedy refused to promise that the USA

SOURCE F

WE HAD TO PREVENT THE USA FROM INTERFERING IN THE CARIBBEAN. THE LOGICAL ANSWER WAS MISSILES. I HAD THE IDEA OF INSTALLING MISSILES WITH NUCLEAR WARHEADS IN CUBA WITHOUT LETTING THE USA FIND OUT THEY WERE THERE UNTIL IT WAS TOO LATE TO DO ANYTHING ABOUT THEM. WE HAD NO DESIRE TO START A WAR.

N S Khrushchev, 1971. (Quoted in his auto-biography **Khrushchev Remembers**.)

SOURCE G

IT IS AN IRONICAL BUT ACCURATE FACT THAT THE TWO STRONGEST POWERS ARE THE TWO IN THE MOST DANGER OF DEVASTATION... WE ARE BOTH CAUGHT UP IN A VICIOUS AND DANGEROUS CYCLE IN WHICH SUSPICION ON ONE SIDE BREEDS SUSPICION ON THE OTHER AND NEW WEAPONS BEGET COUNTER WEAPONS.

John F Kennedy, 1963. (Quoted in Kegley and Wittkopf, **World Politics — Trend and Transformation**.)

---

would not invade Cuba. However agreements between the superpowers were honoured.

2 Kennedy's prestige was greatly enhanced. He had shown firm resolve in a crisis where his Secretary of State, Dean Rusk, spoke of the two sides standing 'eyeball to eyeball'. Kennedy had not blinked.

3 Khrushchev was criticised by China for being foolish enough to put the missiles into Cuba and then for backing down. However, in his memoirs, he took the view that in getting the missiles out of Turkey, and in protecting Cuba, he had achieved "a spectacular success without having to fire a single shot!"

4 Castro remained in power and a thorn in America's side.

5 The crisis demonstrated the dangers of forcing leaders to act under pressure of circumstance, without having time to reflect upon their decisions. It showed how both superpowers needed to avoid direct conflict, and how communications between them needed to be improved. This led to the **hot-line — a** direct telephone link established between the White House and the Kremlin in 1963.

6 Having recognised that their possession of nuclear weapons led to stalemate between them in Cuba, the way was paved for better East-West relations. Nuclear weapons as a deterrent became the main focus of the arms race after 1962 (Source G).

The Cuban missile crisis led to arms control, firstly by the signing of the **Partial Nuclear Test Ban Treaty of 1963**, which forbade atmospheric and underwater testing, though not underground tests. Later, in **1969**, the superpowers agreed to the **Treaty** on the **Non-Proliferation of Nuclear Weapons**.

The threat of a nuclear war in 1962 was frightening enough, but recent revelations show that, to some extent, the threat was avoided as much through good luck as sound judgement. As Robert Mc Namara said in 1992:

"The actions of all three parties were shaped by misjudgment, miscalculations, and misinformation."

The crisis may have contributed to Khrushchev's downfall in 1964, but it also promoted 'peaceful co-existence' and prepared the way for **détente** (unit 2.4).

?

1 Make a timeline of events from 1961 to 1963.

2 If Kennedy and Khrushchev had met for a televised debate in 1963, how would each have defended his actions during 1962?

3 List the reasons for describing the Cuban Missile Crisis as "the most dangerous confrontation of the Cold War".

4 Look at sources D and E. How is the crisis represented in each cartoon and why? How reliable are these representations?

5 How useful is source F as evidence about the crisis?

2.1 VIETNAM

Vietnam, together with Laos and Cambodia formed the French colony of **Indo China**. During the Second World War, Vietnam was occupied by the Japanese who were resisted by Vietnamese nationalists called the **Viet Minh**. When Japan was defeated in 1945 the French tried to take over again but the Vietnamese wanted their independence and fighting continued, this time between the French and the Viet Minh. Despite American funding the French suffered a major defeat at Dien Bien Phu in 1954 and the United Nations tried to reach a peace settlement at the Geneva Conference.

As a result Vietnam was divided along the 17th parallel and it was intended to hold elections in both North and South Vietnam in 1956. By then America had replaced France as the Western power in South Vietnam. The communists had so much support throughout the country that the United States did not encourage elections to be held in the South. Instead the Americans supported **Ngo Dinh Diem** who was a nationalist and a Catholic, unlike most of his fellow countrymen who were Buddhist. Diem stayed in power until 1963 thanks to tough measures against opponents and more than one billion dollars of American aid. Meanwhile, in North Vietnam, a communist government was set up by **Ho Chi Minh**, the nationalist leader, whose aim was to reunite his country. Consequently the guerrilla warfare which had proved so successful when used against the French was continued against Diem's anti-communist government in South Vietnam. US involvement increased gradually so that by the end of 1960 there were 16,000 American advisers in the South.

A *US infantry squad walking through jungle in S Vietnam, half a mile from the Cambodian border. Fifteen minutes after this picture was taken, five of the men were wounded, two of them nearly dead.*

Why did the USA get more involved in Vietnam?

1 Presidents Eisenhower, Kennedy and Johnson all supported the policy of containment. The spread of communism had to be stopped at all costs, and Eisenhower's 'domino theory' speech of 1954 directly referred to Asia. Kennedy saw the influence of communist China and the USSR behind North Vietnam's · continued attacks upon the South and wanted to teach them that their so-called 'wars of liberation' would not succeed in an area that America regarded as vital to her interests. In 1956 he said Vietnam was "the cornerstone of the free world in south-east Asia." Such views led US presidents to support a South Vietnamese government for which they had little respect.

2 South Vietnam was a useful satellite because it was rich in tungsten, tin and rubber.

3 The Americans underestimated both the determination and military expertise of the **National Liberation Front (NLF)** which was formed in 1960. The NLF planned to overthrow Diem's government and assassinated him in 1963, just three weeks before Kennedy was shot in Dallas. The Americans, who called the NLF **Vietcong**, refused to believe that they could be defeated by "a bunch of guerrillas in black pyjamas" from what **Lyndon Johnson** described as a "fourth-rate, raggedy ass little country." Like Kennedy, Johnson was convinced that America's vast wealth and power would ensure victory in any war which was fought by 'conventional' means (ie non-nuclear).

4 Increasingly US pride and honour were at stake in Vietnam. As more troops were sent from 1965 onwards, there was a greater need for victory. When it finally became clear that there would be no victory, the priority was to find a way of ending the war without appearing to be defeated. This was one of the main reasons for the heavy bombing of North Vietnamese cities like **Hanoi** in 1972.

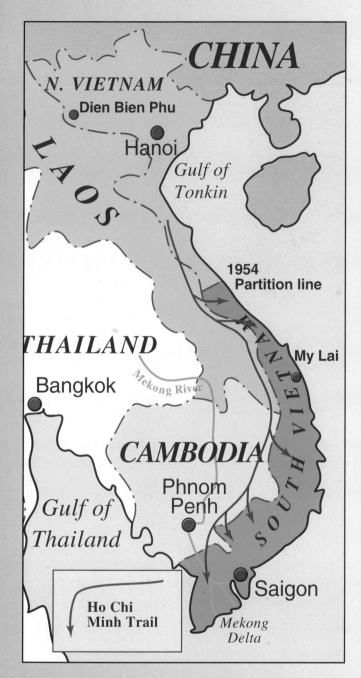

CHINA

N. VIETNAM

Dien Bien Phu

LAOS

Hanoi

Gulf of Tonkin

1954 Partition line

THAILAND

Bangkok

Mekong River

SOUTH VIETNAM

My Lai

CAMBODIA

Phnom Penh

Gulf of Thailand

Ho Chi Minh Trail

Saigon

Mekong Delta

THE VIETNAM WAR

1960	National Liberation Front formed. Aim: Reunite Vietnam.
1963	South Vietnamese President Diem assassinated by NLF.
1964	Gulf of Tonkin Incident which increased American involvement.
1965	North Vietnam bombed in 'Operation Rolling Thunder'.
1968	Tet Offensive in January. My Lai massacre in March. Details became public in 1971 at Lieutenant William Calley's court martial.
1970	Nixon sent troops into Cambodia to clean out Vietcong.
1973	Cease fire agreement between North Vietnam and USA.
1975	South Vietnam defeated. War ended. Country reunited.

the war as he pleased without consulting Congress. Armed with these powers President Johnson ordered air strikes against North Vietnam and in March 1965 sent American troops into South Vietnam to prevent its collapse.

America's longest war 1965-1973

Although Johnson wanted a quick victory he insisted upon fighting a limited war such as America had fought in Korea. This was because he did not want to lose public support nor did he want to risk a war with China and the USSR. Consequently US strategy failed to discourage the North Vietnamese who were prepared to endure heavy losses to achieve their aim of a reunited country.

By 1968 there were over 500,000 US troops in Vietnam but their military strength was weakened by a number of factors.

1 They were mostly inexperienced soldiers whose tour of duty lasted for one year. If they survived the first few months they gradually acquired the necessary military skills only to be sent home again.

2 They were fighting the Vietcong, an expert and experienced guerrilla force who knew the terrain, had high morale and was supported by many civilians. That was essential, as one Vietcong leader admitted: "The people are the water, our armies are the fish".

The Tonkin Resolution 1964

The immediate cause of increased US involvement in the war was the **Gulf of Tonkin** incident in **August 1964**, when North Vietnamese gunboats fired upon the *Maddox*, a US destroyer. At the time the Americans claimed this was a hostile act which was in no way justified. In fact the US destroyer was supporting covert operations in North Vietnam. American outrage led to the **Tonkin Resolution** being passed in Congress by a vote of 48 to 2. This gave the President the right to use "all necessary measures" in the war and was compared to "grandma's nightshirt" because "it covered everything". The President could now conduct

3 They lacked the support of the Vietnamese people who were strongly nationalist and had no reason to support the harsh governments of Diem and his successors. The Americans made no effort to win the hearts and minds of civilians and as their troops faced up to the grim reality of guerrilla warfare, where danger was ever present and the enemy elusive or invisible, they began to treat all civilians as Vietcong suspects. The result was that they lost most of the support they had ever had. In their 'search and destroy' missions the 'body count' became all-important and, as US journalists revealed in horrific detail from 1965 onwards, the bodies were frequently those of old men, women and children, slaughtered in an excess of fear and rage against an unseen enemy. The **My Lai massacre** of **March 1968** was the most infamous example of this (see page 41, bottom right). The Americans killed over 300 people, but recovered only three guns and found no Vietcong in the village.

4 US reliance upon bombing raids was misguided. North Vietnam did not have the kind of industrialised economy which could be destroyed by bombing and the raids had little effect on the Vietcong since it was like "trying to weed a garden with a bulldozer".

The Tet Offensive January 1968

The Tet Offensive was the biggest attack launched by the Vietcong. Using the advantage of surprise, over 70,000 troops attacked 100 towns in South Vietnam, including **Saigon**, the capital. Targets included the US embassy, the Presidential Palace and the Saigon radio station. The Vietcong were driven back and suffered heavy losses. However the Tet Offensive marks a turning point in the war because :-

• Though a military defeat, it was a political success for the Vietcong.
• The unexpected scale of the attack was a blow to US prestige, the attacks in Saigon being particularly humiliating.
• As a result the US lost the will to fight.
• Johnson lost a lot of public confidence and support and announced his decision not to stand for re-election to the Presidency
• Peace negotiations began though they made no progress until late in 1972.
• The US adopted the policy of **Vietnamisation**

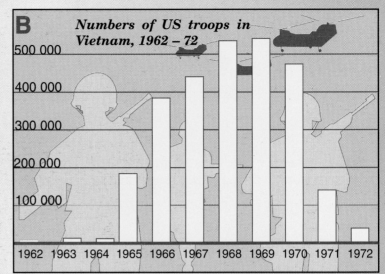

B **Numbers of US troops in Vietnam, 1962 – 72**

in 1969, in which US troops were gradually withdrawn. They hoped that South Vietnam would be strong enough to defend itself. By the end of 1971 there were only 157,000 Americans left in Vietnam.

The role of China and the USSR

Despite their shared ideology China and the USSR played different roles in the war. The Soviet Union was the major supplier of military aid such as arms and missiles as well as petroleum. China was the supply route through which they were delivered to North Vietnam. However, Hanoi had to try to maintain neutrality in the quarrel between China and the USSR which worsened in the late 1960s.

At first the Soviets tended to urge peace while China encouraged North Vietnam to fight on in its 'War of Liberation'. However, when the Americans became hopelessly bogged down in the war, the USSR's international image improved by contrast and its position was strengthened. Consequently the Soviets regarded America's continued involvement in the war as desirable. The longer the war lasted, the greater the humiliation for the West. Lack of progress in peace talks before 1972 was therefore partly due to Soviet reluctance to bring their satellite, North Vietnam, to the negotiating table.

In their dealings with their arch rival the Americans realised that they could not negotiate from a position of strength until they got out of Vietnam. As a result Nixon decided to exploit the Sino-Soviet split and patch up America's long standing quarrel with China (see Chapter 2.3). This in turn contributed to **détente** with the

Soviet Union. As US relations with both China and the USSR began to improve, both communist powers were willing to put pressure on North Vietnam to negotiate.

The end of the war

When **Richard Nixon** became President in January 1969 he was determined to end the war in Vietnam. American opposition to the war had been growing since 1967 and was at its worst in 1970 when four students were shot during an anti-war demonstration at Kent State University, Ohio. Nixon used different approaches to achieve his aim:

American soldiers on a 'search and destroy' mission.

- His policy of Vietnamisation meant passing more responsibility to the South Vietnamese government and armed forces and was designed to get the US out of Vietnam with minimal loss of face. Unfortunately the South Vietnamese had been too dependent upon US support for too long and could not stand alone.
- In 1970 Nixon expanded the war into Cambodia through which ran the so-called **Ho Chi Minh Trail**, the route used by the Vietcong to infiltrate South Vietnam. The bombing of neutral Laos and Cambodia by the Americans was a disaster as it increased support for Communism in both countries.
- Bombing raids over North Vietnamese cities like Hanoi were intensified, partly to compensate for the gradual withdrawal of US troops and partly to pressurise North Vietnam to negotiate.
- By improving diplomatic relations with both China and the Soviet Union, Nixon gained their support in bringing the North Vietnamese to the peace talks.

As a result, a ceasefire was agreed in January 1973. American troops were to be withdrawn and prisoners of war exchanged. Once the Americans left and their POWs had been recovered, Congress stopped all funds to South Vietnam. Meanwhile North Vietnamese troops had been allowed to remain in the South, awaiting elections and reunification, so it was easy for them to launch another attack. The Vietnamese war ended in 1975 with the fall of Saigon and reunification was finally achieved by force. In the same year communist governments were also established in Laos and Cambodia.

The importance of the Vietnam War

1 It was America's longest and costliest war and it ended in military defeat and brought an upsurge in communism in South East Asia which was precisely what a succession of US presidents had wanted to avoid.

2 It proved that in a conventional war even a superpower could be beaten by a sufficiently determined opponent. It taught America a bitter lesson, ie that it should steer clear of conflict unless certain of victory.

3 The policy of containment was undermined since Vietnam showed that America could not defeat communism whenever and wherever it threatened. The Truman Doctrine had promised more than America could deliver. Subsequent events in former Indo-China also raised doubts about the need for American involvement in the first place. Communist China, Cambodia and Vietnam all fought briefly in 1978, demonstrating that nationalism rather than communism was the driving force in South East Asia. In their obsession with containment the Americans had ignored the role of nationalism just as they had ignored the fact that Vietnam was the traditional enemy of China; that the Vietnamese were independent of both the

D

OUR MISSION WAS NOT TO WIN GROUND OR SEIZE POSITIONS, BUT SIMPLY TO KILL. TO KILL COMMUNISTS AND KILL AS MANY OF THEM AS POSSIBLE. STACK 'EM UP LIKE CORDWOOD. VICTORY WAS A HIGH BODY COUNT, DEFEAT A LOW KILL RATIO, WAR A MATTER OF ARITHMETIC. THE PRESSURE ON UNIT COMMANDERS TO PRODUCE ENEMY CORPSES WAS INTENSE AND LED TO SUCH PRACTICES AS COUNTING CIVILIANS AS VIETCONG. "IF IT'S DEAD AND VIETNAMESE, IT'S VIETCONG" WAS A RULE OF THUMB IN THE JUNGLE.

*From **A Rumor of War** by Philip Caputo.*

SOURCE

USSR and China; and that Ho Chi Minh could be as independent a communist leader in Asia as Tito had already proved to be in Europe. Nor was the domino theory an accurate prediction of events. Communism did not spread to Thailand, Burma or Malaya.

4 Vietnam was both a media war and a propaganda disaster. Thanks to the recent developments in satellite communications, news reports and, more importantly, pictures could be transmitted 'live' around the world. The lack of censorship provided opportunities to relay powerful and shocking images of brutality spiralling out of control and made a lasting impression. America's image was tarnished internationally; not one of its European allies helped in Vietnam and France left NATO in 1966.

5 During the war 58,000 US servicemen were killed and it is claimed that many more veterans have committed suicide since the war. There were 300,000 Americans wounded and at least 2,000,000 Vietnamese were killed. More bombs were dropped on Vietnam than throughout Europe in the whole of the Second World War. Landmines continue to claim lives to this day. The use of napalm caused horrific burns and chemicals such as Agent Orange were used to defoliate Vietnam's jungle which provided ideal cover for the Vietcong. Not only was the environmental damage extensive but since Agent Orange contained dioxin it was also responsible for damage to unborn babies and has been linked to cases of cancer among veterans.

E

YOU WALK DOWN A ROAD BETWEEN THE RICE PADDIES. THERE ARE VIETNAMESE IN EVERY PADDY BENT OVER WORKING. NONE OF THEM LOOKS UP WHEN YOU PASS. THEN ALL OF A SUDDEN A MORTAR SHELL LANDS RIGHT IN THE MIDDLE OF THE PATROL AND A COUPLE OF GUYS YOU'VE BEEN BUDDIES WITH ARE DEAD AND A COUPLE OF OTHERS ARE SCREAMING IN AGONY. THE VIETNAMESE ARE STILL WORKING IN THE PADDIES JUST LIKE THEY WERE, AS THOUGH NOTHING AT ALL HAD HAPPENED. DID ONE OF THEM LOB THE MORTAR? IF SO, WHICH ONE? SHOULD YOU KILL ALL OF THEM OR SOME OF THEM?

A US journalist describing the feelings of soldiers.

SOURCE

Vietnam's economy was ruined by the war.

6 Though it was only one contributory factor, Vietnam did pave the way for **détente** and better relations between the superpowers. It also forced the Americans to reassess and improve their relations with China.

?

1 Why did America first become involved in Vietnam?

2 What were the consequences of that involvement?
Complete a table like the one below:

Results affecting ...			
America at home	America abroad	Vietnam	USSR

3 How do sources A, D and E help explain US action in source C?

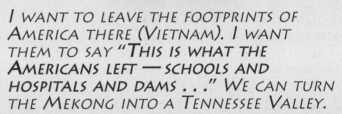

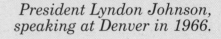

I WANT TO LEAVE THE FOOTPRINTS OF AMERICA THERE (VIETNAM). I WANT THEM TO SAY "THIS IS WHAT THE AMERICANS LEFT — SCHOOLS AND HOSPITALS AND DAMS . . ." WE CAN TURN THE MEKONG INTO A TENNESSEE VALLEY.

President Lyndon Johnson,
speaking at Denver in 1966.

On the night of 20-21 August 1968, a 'tourist' flight from the USSR landed at Prague airport. On board were 52 KGB officials who then took over the control tower so that they could help land the airborne divisions of the Warsaw Pact forces. The action typified the Soviet invasion of Czechoslovakia as it combined efficiency and careful planning with its advantage of surprise. The Czech government recognised the hopelessness of resistance and appealed to the population to act with restraint. Thus the heady days of reform known as the **Prague Spring** came to an end.

Origins of revolution

Since its communist government was established in 1948 Czechoslovakia had been a loyal supporter of the Soviet Union. However, by the mid 1960s there was growing discontent, mainly due to inflation, food shortages and falling living standards, despite the fact that Czechoslovakia had the strongest industry in the Eastern bloc.

When Alexander Dubcek became the new leader of the the Czech communist party in January 1968, he agreed to introduce reforms which would provide 'socialism with a human face'. These reforms were announced in April (see source A below) and were welcomed enthusiastically. As restrictions on freedom of speech were lifted, opponents of the old communist regime could now express their views openly upon the radio and in the newspapers. The early success of the reforms encouraged further demands and there was a mood of optimism everywhere. The easing of so many restrictions became known as the Prague Spring.

Dubcek was anxious not to offend Moscow. As a loyal communist he stressed that Czechoslovakia would remain within the Warsaw Pact and Comecon. Unfortunately these reassurances were not enough to prevent a Soviet invasion of his country.

Reaction within the Eastern Bloc

1 The USSR feared that the liberal ideas of the Prague Spring would spread to other Eastern bloc countries, causing instability and threatening the security of the Soviet Union. In particular it was concerned about the growing trade links between Czechoslovakia and West Germany which it feared would lead to a Western influence in Czechoslovakia which lay in the centre of the Eastern bloc.

2 Poland and East Germany were also anxious to curb what they saw as dangerous developments in Czechoslovakia. They feared the ideas would spread to them causing unrest. Besides, communist leaders in all Eastern bloc countries had many privileges which they would lose if the party's control was weakened.

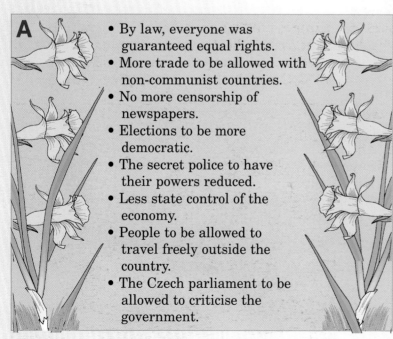

A
- By law, everyone was guaranteed equal rights.
- More trade to be allowed with non-communist countries.
- No more censorship of newspapers.
- Elections to be more democratic.
- The secret police to have their powers reduced.
- Less state control of the economy.
- People to be allowed to travel freely outside the country.
- The Czech parliament to be allowed to criticise the government.

Dubcek's reforms of April 1968.

B

WHEN INTERNAL AND EXTERNAL FORCES HOSTILE TO SOCIALISM ATTEMPT TO TURN THE DEVELOPMENT OF ANY SOCIALIST COUNTRY IN THE DIRECTION OF THE CAPITALIST SYSTEM, WHEN A THREAT ARISES TO THE CAUSE OF SOCIALISM IN THAT COUNTRY, A THREAT TO THE SOCIALIST COMMONWEALTH AS A WHOLE — IT BECOMES NOT ONLY A PROBLEM FOR THE PEOPLE OF THAT COUNTRY BUT ALSO A GENERAL PROBLEM, THE CONCERN OF ALL SOCIALIST COUNTRIES.

The Brezhnev Doctrine

SOURCE

3 At first President Leonid Brezhnev tried to reason with Dubcek, who found himself in a dilemma. If he tried to backtrack on his reforms he would be criticized by the Czechs. If he pressed on, he risked confrontation with the USSR. However Dubcek decided that in 1968 the Soviet Union was unlikely to use force, as they had in Hungary in 1956.

4 In late July 1968 Soviet leaders met Dubcek and reached agreement. This meant that the subsequent invasion came as an even greater shock to Dubcek and his supporters.

Soviet tanks in the streets of Prague.

The invasion

Though five members of the Warsaw Pact were involved (USSR, Poland, Hungary, East Germany and Bulgaria), by far the greatest number of tanks and troops were supplied by the USSR. Altogether 400,000 troops moved into Czechoslovakia in the night of 20/21 August. Preparations had been carefully disguised as part of a series of military exercises all over Eastern Europe and NATO radar stations in West Germany were jammed. The invasion appears to have been deliberately timed before the Czech Communist Party conference which was due to be held in September and was expected to support Dubcek's reforms.

Brezhnev justified the invasion in a speech which became known as the **Brezhnev Doctrine** (source B). He said that if the government in any communist country attempted to make capitalist reforms, then other communist countries should act together to prevent this happening.

Czech reaction

The Czech government was anxious to avoid bloodshed and urged restraint. Consequently there was no popular uprising. Instead, the Czechs adopted **passive resistance**. They refused to cooperate with the Soviet troops and jeered and chanted at the invaders, daubed walls with anti-Soviet slogans and painted out all signposts except those pointing to Moscow!

Results of the invasion

- Dubcek was summoned to Moscow but was reinstated. However, within a year he had been demoted and ended up working in a forestry office for the next twenty years.
- After years of loyal support for the USSR, the Czechs now felt bitter and resentful of Soviet control. Protests continued into 1969. One student set fire to himself in January 1969.
- The reforms were reversed and the communist system was restored.
- China criticised the use of force against fellow communists while Romania refused to co-operate with the USSR and, after 1968, took an increasingly independent line, like Yugoslavia.
- The revival of traditional Cold War tactics was a setback for détente and the US cancelled a summit.

Hungary 1956 and Czechoslovakia 1968

Inevitably the Soviet reaction to reforms in Czechoslovakia revived memories of Hungary in 1956. Certainly there were common factors:

43

SOURCE   A street cartoon in Prague, 1968

- Economic difficulties contributed to both 'revolutions'.
- Force was used by the USSR on both occasions.
- It was clear that the Soviets still considered control of Eastern bloc countries was vital to their security.
- On both occasions the West did nothing more than protest — thanks to Suez and later, Vietnam.

But there were important differences too:

1 In 1956 Hungary was ready to leave the Warsaw Pact. In 1968 Dubcek repeatedly stressed Czechoslovakia's desire to remain within the Pact.

2 In 1956 only Soviet troops were used to crush the uprising because Khrushchev did not trust the Warsaw Pact countries enough to ask for their assistance. In 1968 four of the Warsaw Pact countries sent troops into Czechoslovakia.

3 There was relatively little fighting in 1968 thanks to the government's recommendation of passive resistance. As a result, only 73 Czechs were killed compared with nearly 30,000 Hungarians in 1956.

4 Dubcek and the other leaders were arrested in 1968, but the massive demonstrations of support for them ensured that they were not executed. Indeed Dubcek remained in government for a time, until it was considered safe to dismiss him. In 1956 Nagy was seized by the Soviets, while he was under Yugoslav protection, and was executed. Clearly the Soviets were more influenced by international opinion in 1968 than they were in 1956.

5 In 1956 the USSR had consulted with China before invading Hungary. This was not repeated in 1968 and indeed China was one of the harshest critics of the Soviet action in Czechoslovakia.

Its action in Czechoslovakia made the USSR appear strong and the Eastern bloc united. However, the Czech experiment of 'socialism with a human face' took place because the Soviet grip on its satellites had begun to weaken. Brezhnev's firm handling of the crisis did not prevent Romania from following a more independent foreign policy, nor did it prevent the first strikes in Poland in 1970. Such developments worried Soviet leaders, but the growing friendship between the USA and China caused greater concern.

?

1 Read source A. Why would Dubcek's reforms of 1968 have worried the Soviets?

2 What point was the cartoonist making in source D? Is source D reliable as evidence? Explain your answer.

3 "Soviet policy in Eastern Europe had not changed between 1956 and 1968." Do you agree? Give reasons for your answer.

2.3 CHINA AND THE SUPERPOWERS

The proclamation of the **People's Republic of China** in October 1949 marked the end of a long drawn out civil war between the Nationalist army of Chiang Kai-shek and the Communists, whose leader was **Mao Zedong**. After years of Japanese occupation, followed by renewed civil war, China was in a terrible state. The country was backward, its people poor, its industry almost non-existent. Unemployment was high, inflation was rising rapidly and famine threatened. The world's newest communist government needed help and the most obvious source of aid was the USSR.

Despite Mao's support among the Chinese people, Stalin had agreed in 1945 to the reinstatement of **Chiang Kai-shek** as ruler of China. However Mao's ultimate success was hailed as a victory for communism and the two countries signed a **Treaty of Friendship** in **February 1950**. The treaty was meant to last 30 years and the USSR promised to lend 300 million dollars to China to aid recovery. By 1960 disagreements had erupted into an open quarrel, which led to the withdrawal of Soviet advisers and left projects, such as factories, unfinished. Both countries criticised each other and, by 1967, the Beijing press was referring to Soviet leaders like Khrushchev and Brezhnev as 'scabs'.

Why was there a Sino-Soviet split?

Firstly, China was dissatisfied with the aid received and industrial recovery was slow. As far as the Chinese were concerned, the USSR proved to be a false friend. It refused to give China the hydrogen bomb in 1958 and, though willing to install nuclear weapons on Chinese soil, insisted they should remain under Soviet control. This was because Mao had displayed an alarming lack of concern about the dangers of a nuclear war. Nor were the Soviets prepared to help China against Taiwan (eg in the attack upon nearby offshore islands in 1955). As a result China was forced to develop its own nuclear weapons. It refused to sign the **Nuclear Test Ban Treaty of 1963** and went on to explode its first atomic bomb in October 1964.

Secondly, ideological differences emerged about the same time as China began to feel let down by the USSR. Khrushchev detected signs of disagreement as early as 1954, when he and other Soviet leaders visited Beijing (source A).

The turning point was Khrushchev's famous speech of 1956 denouncing Stalin and calling for peaceful co-existence with the West. This was done without discussion with China. Mao disagreed with the criticism of Stalin and saw the call for co-existence as a betrayal of Marx and Lenin. China wanted the USSR to support 'wars of liberation'. Disenchantment led to the new economic policy known as the **Great Leap Forward**. This was Mao's attempt to make China independent of Soviet aid, but the Soviets criticised the reliance upon manpower rather than technology (source B).

The Soviets proved correct as the Great Leap Forward's initial success in increasing steel production turned rapidly to failure, when the lack of skill produced iron which was brittle and virtually useless. By 1959 there was famine in China too, as food production continued to lag behind. Mao's **Cultural Revolution** of **1966-69** also highlighted differences. This was an attempt to inject enthusiasm into the communist revolution and was aimed deliberately at the

A *EVER SINCE I'VE FIRST MET MAO, I'VE KNOWN... THAT MAO WOULD NEVER BE ABLE TO RECONCILE HIMSELF TO ANY OTHER COMMUNIST PARTY BEING IN ANY WAY SUPERIOR TO HIS OWN WITHIN THE WORLD COMMUNIST MOVEMENT...*

*Nikita Khrushchev, in **Khrushchev Remembers**, 1970.*

SOURCE

young. The slogan **'to rebel is justified'** did not appeal to the USSR, whose reaction to moderate reform in Czechoslovakia in 1968 was to intervene and restore the old system. The open hostility between the leading communist countries was clearly demonstrated when the Soviet embassy was besieged during the Cultural Revolution. Moscow also resented China's role as an important leader of international communism in the Third World by the late 1960s.

Thirdly, a number of disputes between China and the USSR drew attention to their fundamental differences.

1 Khrushchev's climbdown over Cuba was roundly condemned by China, which became convinced that the USSR would never again risk such a confrontation with the USA. China had to look after itself — hence its development of the atom bomb.

2 During a border war between China and India, in 1962, Moscow was officially neutral, but provided India with jet engines for its military aircraft.

3 A more serious border dispute developed between China and the USSR between 1964 and 1969. This was rooted in the 19th century expansion of Tsarist Russia, and China wanted its territory returned. The most dangerous incident occurred in March 1969 when 31 Soviets were killed (Chinese casualty figures are unknown). Despite its huge population, China remained at a disadvantage militarily. Nevertheless, border tensions forced the Soviets to maintain a strong force in the region. In 1972 it was estimated that over 1 million Soviet troops, 10,000 tanks and over 1000 aircraft were deployed on the border with China.

4 The Brezhnev Doctrine, which was the result of the crisis in Czechoslovakia, seemed to threaten China too, especially when it had such a serious border dispute with the USSR and was at loggerheads over ideology as well.

Chinese villagers producing steel in their own furnaces during the 'Great Leap Forward' in the late 1950s. A Chinese propaganda picture.

China and the USA

By 1969 the Americans were finally willing to exploit the Sino-Soviet split and explore the possibilities of friendship with Communist China. This represented a major turning point in US foreign policy.

Since 1949 America and China had been hostile. The major cause of their quarrel (apart from ideology) was **Taiwan**. The USA supported Chiang Kai-shek and gave him financial and military assistance. During the Korean war Taiwan became a US military base and a treaty, signed in 1955, committed a US fleet to the protection of Taiwan. The Americans also kept Communist China out of the UN, where Nationalist China (ie Taiwan) continued to hold a seat. The dispute over Taiwan led to China shelling offshore islands nearby and the US threatened retaliation with nuclear weapons, which forced China to back down.

Americans perceived Communist China as an 'international outlaw' and the main supporter of communist activities in SE Asia (eg Korea and later Vietnam). China believed the US was trying to isolate it, not only by excluding it from the UN, but also by a ban on all trade and travel links between their countries. Nevertheless the Korean war taught both countries to be more cautious in their dealings with each other. For instance, in 1965 they agreed that the US would not invade North Vietnam so that there was no danger of direct confrontation.

46

'Playing the China card'

Occasionally during the 1950s and early 1960s American statesmen considered making common cause with the Soviets against China, but never did so. The idea of making common cause with China was entirely new. Both countries could see the benefits.

President Nixon meeting mao Zedong.

- President Nixon wanted to withdraw from Vietnam and needed diplomatic support from China (one of North Vietnam's backers) to get North Vietnam to negotiate.
- By exploiting the Sino-Soviet split the US could get China's support against the USSR.
- Friendship with China could open up new markets for American industry.
- Since the Tet Offensive of 1968 China regarded the USSR as the stronger superpower, and therefore the biggest threat. If China and America became friends, China would have US support against the USSR.
- China recognised that a shared ideology did not guarantee agreement. Indeed different visions of the same ideology caused sharp disagreement. China saw advantages in steering a more independent line and as America had no shared border it offered no immediate territorial threat.
- China wanted Western technology and investment to improve its industry.

Results

1 Friendly contacts brought an invitation to the US table tennis team to visit Beijing in 1971. 'Ping pong diplomacy' in turn led to China's admission to the UN in October 1971 and Nixon's own visit to China in February 1972 in "the week that changed the world" as he modestly put it.

2 In the **Friendship Treaty** of **1972** both countries renounced any ambitions to dominate SE Asia. Washington agreed to withdraw its troops from Taiwan. (No firm date was set.) Full diplomatic recognition of China followed in 1978.

3 The improved relationship contributed to the ending of America's war in Vietnam.

4 China placed 2 billion dollars worth of orders for machinery etc, with the USA.

5 While Nixon personally warmed to the Chinese Prime Minister, **Zhou Enlai**, in a way he had

not to Brezhnev, some of his satisfaction from his achievement came from the fact that his visit put pressure on the Soviets to fix a date for a summit that same year. The triangular relationship between China, America and the USSR meant no-one wanted to be the odd one out. Consequently the Soviets were now keener to improve relations with America too.

?

1 Summarise the reasons for the Sino-Soviet split in a web diagram.

2 (a) What were the main causes of disagreement between China and the USA?
(b) List the advantages each expected to gain from their friendship.

3 Make a timeline to chart China's relationship with both superpowers between 1949 and 1978.

American cartoon about the reasons for Salt, published in 1970.

A

B

EVEN AN ECONOMY SUCH AS THAT OF THE USA COULD NOT AFFORD GUNS, BUTTER AND A WELFARE STATE ALL AT THE SAME TIME.

Martin Walker **The Cold War**, *1993.*

SOURCE

The 1970s were the decade of **détente**. This meant an easing of tensions between the two superpowers and was marked by a number of agreements, the most important of which aimed to control the arms race (see table). These, together with more frequent meetings between the leaders of the USA and USSR increased co-operation and helped to develop trade links between the two countries. Why, after 25 years of Cold War, did relations appear to improve so dramatically?

Reasons for Détente

By 1970, while both superpowers had their own reasons for supporting détente, they also faced similar problems.

1 Both feared a nuclear war and as the new **anti-ballistic missiles (ABMs)** could now protect their cities from attack, **MAD** was out of date as a policy of deterrence.

2 Both needed to slow down the arms race because they were worried about the crippling costs. ABMs were very expensive and the Americans had recently developed **multiple independently targeted re-entry vehicles (MIRVs)** which the Soviets would have to copy. Leonid Brezhnev had increased defence budgets and consequently the Soviets had started to catch up with the USA. For the first time the Soviets could negotiate as equals in any arms talks.

3 Both faced economic problems. Though the USSR produced more coal, oil and steel than the USA, and American cars and textiles could no longer compete in world markets, the Soviets needed Western industrial and computer technology. They also needed grain. Farmers in the USSR were only a sixth as productive as American farmers. Though less than 3% of Soviet land was privately owned, it produced nearly 40% of the country's meat, dairy produce and vegetables. The failure of the 1972 grain harvest meant Western aid was urgently needed, just when the USA itself needed new markets. In 1971 America had a trade deficit in manufactured goods for the first time since 1945 and inflation was rising (source B).

4 Both found it difficult to control their satellites and traditional power blocs. The US defence of South Vietnam proved both expensive and unpopular, and defeat made Americans more anxious to avoid war. The USA could no longer depend upon its Cold War allies for support either. For instance, no NATO country helped America in Vietnam. Western Europe was also taking a more independent line. **Willy Brandt**, the new West German Chancellor in 1969, began talks with both the Soviets and East Germans. His policy of **Ostpolitik** (Eastern policy) laid the foundation for détente in Europe. The events in Czechoslovakia in 1968 and the worsening border conflict with China

THE MAIN AGREEMENTS DURING DÉTENTE			
Date	**Agreement**	**Countries**	**Summary of agreement**
August 1970	Moscow Treaty	USSR and West Germany	West Germany accepted the division of Germany and the loss of German territory to Poland and the USSR in 1945.
September 1971	Final Quadripartite Protocol	USSR and West Germany	The USSR recognised the ties between West Germany and West Berlin
May 1972	SALT I (a) Interim Treaty	USSR & USA	Agreement limited number of ICBMs, SLBMs and bombers for five years (MIRVs excluded at US request).
	(b) ABM Treaty	USSR & USA	Each side limited to two ABM sites of no more than 100 missile launchers.
	Trade agreement	USSR & USA	Soviets settled war debts to the USA. In return USSR purchased US technology on credit and $1 billion worth of agricultural products. Cheap grain was the most important. The wheat deal alone doubled US – Soviet trade
December 1972	Basic Treaty	East Germany West Germany	Both accepted the existence of two German states.
August 1975	Helsinki Agreement	All European countries, USA and Canada	The USSR got recognition of its sphere of influence, through acceptance of existing borders within Europe, and the USA got Soviet agreement to respect human rights – eg freedom of speech – (in so-called 'Basket 3').
June 1979	SALT II	USA and USSR	Agreed a maximum of 2400 missile launchers. Never ratified due to Soviet invasion of Afghanistan.

showed that the USSR had its own problems, both in controlling its satellites and in asserting its authority throughout the communist world. Tough action in Czechoslovakia failed either to stop Romania from pursuing its own policies, or to prevent riots in Poland in 1970.

5 While their authority was increasingly challenged abroad, both superpowers had to deal with growing criticism at home. From 1968 onwards Soviet dissidents seemed as big a problem to the Kremlin as the anti-Vietnam demonstrators and Civil Rights movement were to the White House.

Expectations of Détente

Neither superpower expected détente to lead to lasting peace, though the general public tended to be more hopeful. The Americans feared the growth of Soviet power and influence, and believed that détente would be a way of reducing superpower rivalry and controlling Soviet ambitions. They hoped to bargain with the Soviets. If the USSR co-operated in one area, such as Vietnam, by pressurising North Vietnam to negotiate, it would be rewarded with a deal on arms control or cheap grain. Détente was containment in a different form.

The Soviets saw détente as a means of stabilising the arms race, reducing defence costs and leaving them free to increase their power and influence elsewhere, especially in the Third World. While the Soviets were worried by the growing friendship between China and America, and saw détente as a way of getting US support against China, the Americans viewed détente as a means of keeping communist China and the USSR apart.

How successful was Détente?

1 In Europe the division of Germany ceased to be an issue and West Berlin ceased to be a trouble spot. The longstanding quarrels arising from the occupation of Germany in 1945 were finally settled and there would be no repetition of the crises of 1948 and 1961.

2 There was greater co-operation in some areas. For example, the Soviets did exert some pressure on North Vietnam to come to terms thus ending US involvement in Vietnam. As part of the agreement on scientific co-operation US and Soviet astronauts met in space in **1975** in the **Apollo-Soyuz link-up**.

3 During détente, America continued to benefit from the quarrel between China and the USSR. Both were anxious to maintain friendly relations with the US and avoid isolation.

4 US trade increased with both China and the USSR. Initially the sale of cheap American grain caused some grumbling about the 'Great Grain Robbery', which created shortages at home, raised prices and worsened inflation. However, US farmers benefited so much from these exports that, when President **Jimmy Carter** cut sales in 1980 to punish the USSR for invading Afghanistan, farmers persuaded President **Ronald Reagan**'s government to restore them in 1981. As the Soviet economy continued to stagnate, the USSR became increasingly dependent upon the West.

5 The agreements on arms control were less successful. They did end the race to build expensive ABMs but the limits in the **Interim Agreement** were set relatively high and the omission of **MIRVs** from **Salt I** meant both superpowers would deploy more of these. MIRVs contained multiple warheads capable of hitting widely separated areas. One US submarine fitted with MIRVs had the same firepower as 160 Hiroshima bombs. In 1972 the US had 30 submarines armed with MIRVs. By the mid 1970s the USSR also had MIRVs and by 1979 the US government believed that the Soviets were ahead in the arms race.

6 The **Helsinki Agreement** never lived up to Western expectations. There was no real improvement in human rights in Eastern Europe and the West lacked the means to enforce the pledges of 1975. Frustration with the Soviets' continuing poor record on human rights caused Carter to delay signing **Salt II**. Nevertheless, by signing these pledges the USSR led dissidents to expect reforms within the Eastern bloc. Such expectations would have to be resisted or fulfilled and, in either case, would bring pressure for change.

Despite criticisms, détente did bring about a thaw in the Cold War. The fact that the superpowers reached any agreement on arms control was itself an achievement and did much to reduce international tensions for a time. By reducing East-West tension, détente encouraged a variety of views on both sides of the iron curtain. Thanks to détente, the superpowers increasingly tried to solve disputes through negotiation and, to a large extent, this approach survived the renewal of Cold War after 1979.

Jimmy Carter and Leonid Brezhnev during a break in the SALT II discussions in Vienna, June 1979.

?

1 According to source A, why did the superpowers begin talks on arms limitation?

2 Summarise the reasons for détente as shown below:

American reasons	Soviet reasons

3 Which were the most successful agreements of détente and why?
Which were the least successful agreements and why?

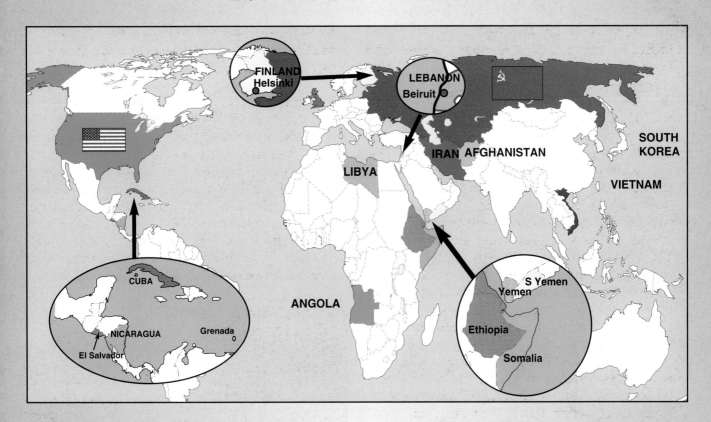

The Soviet invasion of **Afghanistan** on Christmas Eve 1979, marked the end of détente. However détente had had its critics for some time, especially in the West, where it was perceived as an arrangement which benefited the Soviets far more than anyone else (source A). Ronald Reagan expressed American disillusionment with détente in 1976 (source B).

Supporters of détente could draw attention to the gains made for human rights at Helsinki but the arrest of Soviet dissidents, who tried to monitor Soviet progress on human rights, meant such a defence had a hollow ring.

American dissatisfaction with détente appeared as early as 1973 when suspicions were aroused over Soviet intentions in the Middle East. In 1975 the Soviet satellite, North Vietnam, overran the South, which no longer had American protection. When civil war broke out in the former Portuguese colony of Angola in 1975, Soviet planes brought 12,000 Cuban troops to intervene on behalf of their side in the dispute. Victory in Angola was swiftly followed by similar intervention (Soviet arms, Cuban soldiers) in the civil war in Ethiopia, where left-wing forces were also successful by 1977. Soviet arms and support helped the communist forces of **North Yemen** to take over **South Yemen** in 1978. Though the USSR gained little, in the long term, from these overseas exploits, its successes underlined the comparative weakness of its rival America.

When war broke out between **Ethiopia** and **Somalia** in 1977, the superpowers had supported different sides but in neither Angola or Somalia did the USA match the efforts of the USSR and Cuba. This was due to the combined effects of defeat in Vietnam and the Watergate scandal which forced President Nixon to resign in 1974. Nixon's downfall weakened the Presidency at a time when Brezhnev provided stable leadership in the USSR and brought greater caution in American foreign policy with a marked reluctance to risk conflict. After Vietnam the US Congress refused to allow intervention in Angola, and so

A détente is... ...the exchange of sweet nothings.

détente is... covering up his treaty violations.

détente is... ...knowing when to give something for nothing

British newspaper cartoon from 1976. The two figures are Henry Kissinger, US Secretary of State, and Loenid Brezhnev, the Soviet leader.

left the USSR free to act. While US confidence dipped, the Soviets could exploit their recently developed capability to mount military operations far from home and take advantage of any opportunity to extend their influence.

Concern about the extent of Soviet ambitions in the Third World was matched by a growing fear that America was losing the arms race. Due to defence cutbacks by Congress, the USA had fallen behind in certain types of weapons. Since perceptions of military strength were still based upon the number of missiles possessed by each superpower, détente was blamed for the American shortfall. Critics of détente could also point to the latest Soviet threat in Europe where the first **SS-20s** were **deployed in 1976**. These new intermediate range missiles caused anxiety about the state of NATO's European defences and led to the decision in 1979 to place **Cruise** and **Pershing missiles** in NATO countries of Western Europe. The decision led to popular protests in these same countries where people felt the USA was willing to fight a nuclear war providing it was fought in Europe.

1979 was a particularly bad year for America abroad. The overthrow of the **Shah of Iran**, America's staunch ally, by Muslim fundamentalists who were anti-Western, was a major setback, while the discovery of a Soviet combat brigade in Cuba led to a demand for its withdrawal. The demand was ignored, forcing the US government to back down. When the Soviets ignored Carter's warning and invaded Afghanistan at Christmas, it was the final straw.

Afghanistan

Before 1978 Afghanistan was non-aligned, that is, it belonged to a group of neutral countries which did not commit themselves to the support of either superpower. Aid from the Soviet Union did give it more influence within Afghanistan than any other country had, but it was not until after a communist coup in 1978, that Soviet advisers began to arrive in greater numbers.

The new government faced growing opposition from Muslim fundamentalists who were anti-communist and it seems likely that the Soviet decision to send 85,000 troops into Afghanistan, on Christmas Eve, 1979, stemmed from fear that these Muslims would overthrow the communist government. However the Americans suspected a more sinister motive, believing that this was the latest Soviet attempt to gain control of an area within reach of Middle East oil. For instance, neighbouring Iran, into which the USA had poured aid to no effect, and was now under the control of Muslim fundamentalists, was a possible target.

Fear of Soviet expansion in the Middle East was justified by recent Soviet intervention in Ethiopia and South Yemen. For this reason President Carter reacted strongly to the Soviet invasion of Afghanistan, issuing the **Carter Doctrine** (source C), increasing defence budgets, cancelling grain exports and calling for a boycott of the 1980 Moscow Olympics.

The Soviet Union's invasion of Afghanistan was its first major military undertaking outside Europe since 1945, and proved no more successful than Imperial Russia's attempts to control the same region in the 19th century. The mountainous terrain suited the guerrilla tactics used by the Afghans. Casualties mounted, 100,000 troops were committed to the struggle and, ten years later, the Soviets were no closer to success. Afghanistan became a Soviet Vietnam. Like America the USSR found that even superpowers were not guaranteed victory in conventional warfare. Though the invasion was justified by the

52

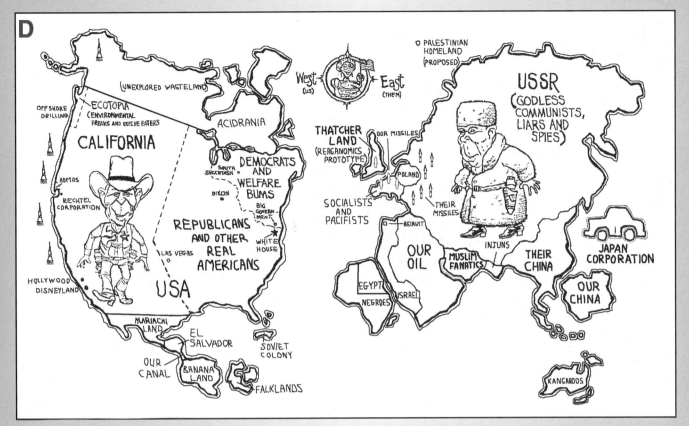

How Ronald Reagan saw the world, from an American cartoon, published in 1982.

Brezhnev Doctrine (see page 42), the war proved costly in many ways. The Soviet Union could not bear the financial burden; it lost support in Third World countries; it destroyed détente and made the Americans refuse to ratify **SALT II**.

President Reagan

Foreign policy featured heavily in the **1980** Presidential campaign and contributed to Ronald Reagan's success. Reagan was "the most unashamedly ideological of post-war Presidents"

(Crockatt). He believed that communism lay at the root of most of the world's problems, and opposed détente, which he blamed for weakening both the US armed forces, and the American will to fight the evils of communism. Reagan wanted to restore US superiority in the superpower conflict. Once in office, defence budgets were further increased and the US took a tougher stance abroad in defence of its interests. Thus, in the struggle against communism, it supported the right-wing government of **El Salvador** and

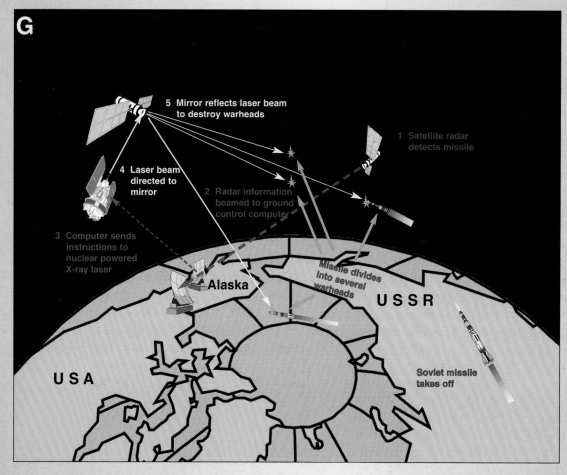

G

5 Mirror reflects laser beam to destroy warheads

1 Satellite radar detects missile

4 Laser beam directed to mirror

2 Radar information beamed to ground control computer

3 Computer sends instructions to nuclear powered X-ray laser

Alaska

Missile divides into several warheads

USSR

USA

Soviet missile takes off

How the Strategic Defence Initiative (Star Wars) worked.

secretly supplied arms to the anti-communist rebels (Contras) in **Nicaragua**; US troops were sent to **Beirut** in **1982** and into **Grenada** in **1983**; and in **1986 Libya** was bombed. However these were limited operations. Reagan's government knew better than to risk another Vietnam.

A New Cold War

To build up America's image abroad after what he saw as the damaging effects of détente, Reagan made a number of tough speeches which were blatantly anti-Soviet (source E). These created the impression that America was an aggressive superpower, an impression which actions such as the bombing of Libya tended to reinforce.

Tensions between the superpowers were high in 1983, the year of Reagan's 'evil empire' speech and his announcement of plans to develop the **Strategic Defence Initiative (SDI)**, popularly nicknamed **'Star Wars'**. Reagan took a personal interest in SDI, which he claimed would replace an offensive system with a defensive one. SDI was a space-based, computer-controlled defence system using lasers to shoot down missiles in space before they could reach their targets. To

work it needed to be totally accurate and reliable, so that all enemy missiles were destroyed. Not one enemy missile could be left undetected.

Scientists were doubtful that this could be done and the huge cost involved meant SDI was soon scaled down, so that instead of replacing the old system, it was added to it. This made the Soviets suspect that the USA was trying to get first strike capability. SDI would protect America from a Soviet attack and so would upset the balance between superpowers. Not only were the Soviets worried, but also America's allies in Europe. They feared Reagan's tough stance, and the arms race, would lead to war and that SDI would leave Western Europe the sole target for Soviet missiles. NATO's first **Cruise and Pershing missiles** were installed in Europe in **November 1983** amidst strong opposition from anti-nuclear campaigners, as at **Greenham Common** in the UK. The Soviet reaction was to walk out of the arms talks.

However the Soviets also contributed to the mounting tensions. In 1981, after Reagan's government had indicated its wish to reopen strategic nuclear talks, Reagan proposed the **'Zero option'**, under which the USA would

54

undertake not to put Cruise and Pershing missiles into Europe, if the USSR removed its SS-20s. The proposal was rejected. In January 1983 on a visit to West Germany, **Gromyko**, the Soviet Foreign Minister, described the US leaders as:

"... *compulsive gamblers and adventurists who declare that they are ready to plunge mankind into a nuclear catastrophe for the sake of their ambitions.*"

KGB officials were told to publicise the slogan 'Reagan means War' throughout Europe. In September 1983 a South Korean passenger aircraft was shot down over the USSR, after it strayed into Soviet airspace. A US Congressman was among the 269 casualties. The Soviet action showed how dangerous tensions were at the time and though there was some improvement in 1984, Moscow boycotted the Los Angeles Olympics.

Yet despite the suspicions, tensions and insults, both superpowers were still willing to negotiate. Though **SALT II** had never been ratified by the US Senate, both America and the USSR observed the agreement beyond its expiry date of 1985. In 1982 negotiations for **Strategic Arms Reduction Talks (START)** began at Geneva. The change of name from **SALT** marked an important development in arms control. Though the talks were broken off late in 1983, they resumed in 1985.

Undoubtedly there was a cooling in East-West relations in the early 1980s. Reagan made no secret of his views on communism, and his aggressive foreign policy contrasted sharply with that of his predecessors, during the decade of détente. His struggle to re-establish America as the dominant superpower was assisted by the fact that his first term as President coincided with rapid changes in the Soviet Presidency, following the **death of Brezhnev** in **November 1982**. However, though Reagan was blamed for bringing about a renewal of Cold War, in his second term of office he proved to be a moving force for peace.

Soviet Presidents 1964-1991

1964 - 1982	Leonid Brezhnev
1983 - 1984	Yuri Andropov
1984 - 1985	Konstantin Chernenko
1985 - 1991	Mikhail Gorbachev

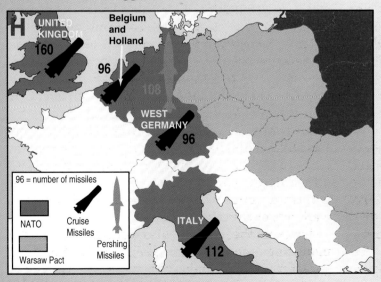

The deployment of Cruise and Pershing missiles in Europe, after 1983.

?

1. (a) How does source B support source A?
   (b) Are sources A and B reliable as evidence on détente?

2. Using sources D, E and F, describe and explain Ronald Reagan's attitude towards the Soviet Union in the early 1980s.

3. Why did SDI raise tensions between the superpowers?

4. Make a timeline of events between 1975 and 1985.

2.6 GORBACHEV AND THE COLLAPSE OF COMMUNISM

Within days of the death of Chernenko in March 1985 **Mikhail Gorbachev** was elected as his successor. At the age of 54 he was one of a new generation of well educated Communists who were too young to remember the grim pre-war years under Stalin. He seemed more Western than his predecessors and, on a visit to London in December 1984, had made a favourable impression upon the British Prime Minister, Margaret Thatcher, who was Reagan's staunchest ally. No-one, including Gorbachev himself, could have foreseen that, within five years, the communist governments of Eastern Europe would be overthrown; that Soviet control of its satellites would be destroyed; and that the Soviet Union itself would be on the verge of disintegration.

Soviet economic problems

The economic problems of the early 1970s had steadily worsened. The Soviet share of world trade fell at a time when East-West trade was increasing as a result of détente. Industrial production and agriculture both showed slow growth. There were food shortages caused by poor transport and distribution so that 30% of the annual harvest was left to rot. The steel industry needed modernisation and Soviet use of micro-electronics and computers lagged well behind that of the USA. For technological, as well as financial, reasons the Soviets could not develop their own **'Star Wars'** defence system.

Under Brezhnev, defence budgets had increased, while health care suffered so that the Soviet Union had an infant mortality rate which was unusually high for a developed country. In Stalin's day people worked hard, either out of fear or loyalty, but now they did not and, while it remained illegal to buy or sell for profit, there was little incentive to work harder. As people became more disillusioned with their system of government, their inability to change it made growing numbers turn to alcohol, drugs, crime and absenteeism.

Under Brezhnev there had been no reform (source A). Instead, the USSR continued to subsidise its oil exports to Eastern Europe, though oil prices slumped in the 1980s. Cuba, Angola, Vietnam and Ethiopia continued to receive Soviet aid, while the war in Afghanistan was a further costly drain on resources. Reagan was right to believe that the USSR could not afford the arms race and Mikhail Gorbachev knew it. He was also aware of the pressing need to modernise industry, improve production and trade figures and that to achieve such aims, major changes had to be made in a country where even a photocopier, never mind a computer, could undermine government control of information.

Gorbachev's solutions

At home his main policies were:

1 **Glasnost** (openness) By encouraging people to speak out and criticise the system, Gorbachev hoped to increase efficiency, to raise morale and to stamp out corruption.

2 **Perestroika** (restructuring and renewal) To revive the Soviet economy, market forces were reintroduced and more control was given to local managers (source B).

Gorbachev realised that if the aims of **perestroika** were to be met, he needed to reduce spending on both the arms race and aid to

WE ARE ENTERING AN ERA IN WHICH PROGRESS WILL BE BASED ON THE COMMON INTERESTS OF THE WHOLE OF HUMANKIND. . . . THIS NEW STAGE REQUIRES THE FREEING OF INTERNATIONAL RELATIONS FROM IDEOLOGY. . . FORCE, OR THE THREAT OF FORCE, NEITHER CAN, NOR SHOULD BE INSTRUMENTS OF FOREIGN POLICY. . . THE PRINCIPLE OF THE FREEDOM OF CHOICE IS VITAL. REFUSAL TO RECOGNISE THIS PRINCIPLE WILL HAVE SERIOUS CONSEQUENCES FOR WORLD PEACE.

Extracts from a speech by Mikhail Gorbachev at the United Nations, 7 December 1988.

SOURCE

Mikhail Gorbachev and Ronald Reagan in Washington, 1987. Also present are their wives Raisa Gorbachev and Nancy Reagan (in red).

satellites, leaving more money to be spent on the Soviet people. Gorbachev's willingness to reach agreement with the West helped bring the Cold War to an end. His views were outlined to the United Nations in December 1988 (source C) and marked a turning point in Soviet relations with the West. Not only did he abandon the traditional view of an ideological conflict between communism and capitalism but also the Brezhnev Doctrine of 1968. Like his other policies these were to have far reaching consequences.

Gorbachev and Reagan

Despite recent tensions between the super-powers, both leaders were anxious to talk about arms control. Their **first summit** took place in **November 1985** at **Geneva**. By then Gorbachev had already replaced Gromyko (nicknamed 'Grim Grom' in America) by his friend, **Eduard Shevardnadze**. The new Foreign Minister told a meeting of Soviet ambassadors, "'We must stop being perceived as Mr Nyet". ('Nyet' is Russian for 'no'.)

Though the Americans remained suspicious of Soviet intentions until 1989, Reagan himself felt that the build-up of US weapons in the early 1980s now allowed America to negotiate from a position of strength. Besides, the US could not afford to retain high defence budgets indefinitely. It already had large debts.

- At the **Geneva summit** the two leaders got on well and, in a joint statement, declared that "a nuclear war cannot be won and must not be fought".

- At **Reykjavik** in **October 1986** proposals went beyond arms reduction to complete disarmament. Though Reagan's refusal to abandon **SDI** prevented any agreement, the summit proved that arms reduction lay within reach.

- At **Washington** in **December 1987**, the **Intermediate Range Nuclear Force Treaty (INF Treaty)** was signed. This historic treaty was the first to reduce weapons and the first to allow inspections of each other's nuclear arsenals. (At the height of the Cold War such inspections would have been unthinkable.) The treaty got rid of **SS-20s** and **Cruise** and **Pershing** missiles just as Reagan proposed in the 'zero option' of 1981.

- In **1988** the Soviets agreed to **withdraw from Afghanistan** (withdrawal completed February 1989). The decision had actually been taken in 1986 and was partly influenced by the Afghan success in destroying Soviet helicopters with Stinger missiles supplied by the USA.

Though discussions at the **Moscow summit** in **May 1988** foundered yet again on the issue of SDI, the goodwill between Reagan and Gorbachev and their respective countries was unharmed. Just as Gorbachev encountered friendly crowds in Washington, chanting 'Gorby, Gorby', so Reagan and the Soviet leader got a similar welcome as they strolled through Red Square. In his speech to the UN in December 1988 Gorbachev also announced a cut of 500,000 men from the Soviet army, and a withdrawal of 50,000 men and 5000 tanks from Eastern

Europe. Meanwhile **SDI** was increasingly criticised within America and ultimately was abandoned by Reagan's successor, **George Bush**.

Gorbachev's policies made him the most popular Soviet leader of all time in the West but, at home, his reform programme did not have the results he intended. Glasnost unleashed criticism of the communist system throughout the Eastern bloc and the release of Soviet dissidents in 1987-8 may have pleased the West but it also added to Gorbachev's difficulties as the opposition now had leaders. Nationalism within the Soviet republics could not have been voiced but for glasnost. In the neighbouring countries of Eastern Europe, where communism had been imposed by the USSR after 1945, glasnost and perestroika weakened the authority of the communist governments and encouraged the growth of opposition. With Gorbachev's public undertaking in December 1988 that the Soviet Union would not intervene in the internal affairs of other countries, the stage was set for revolution.

1989 'The year of miracles'

In the past, critics of communist rule in Eastern Europe had been arrested and silenced. If their own governments could not, or would not, control them, then the Red Army would restore order by force — as in Hungary in 1956 and Czechoslovakia in 1968. The absence of opposition owed more to fear than contentment. Since 1973 Eastern European economies had suffered due to high oil prices. Poland, in particular, had borrowed heavily from the West and acquired huge debts, which it could not repay. Low living standards in the East contrasted unfavourably with the West, whose prosperity could be seen daily on television (West German TV was watched in both East Germany and Czechoslovakia). During détente East-West trade links were developed. Western culture, pop music, etc, became more widely available in Soviet bloc countries, and expectations of freedom were raised by the Helsinki Agreement.

Economic problems, especially food shortages, led to **unrest in Poland** in **1980** and to the

---

1989 — THE YEAR OF MIRACLES

January	Strikes in Poland forced the government to have talks with Solidarity. In Hungary a new law allowed opposition parties to form.
February	*In Bulgaria a free trade union like Solidarity is formed.*
March	Demonstrations in Hungary against occupation by Soviet troops.
April	*In Poland Solidarity was made legal and workers were given the right to strike. The first free elections in Eastern Europe since 1945 are promised.*
May	Demonstrations in Czechoslovakia demanding reform. Hungarians start dismantling barbed wire fence on border with Austria.
June	*Solidarity won all 162 seats which could be contested in the Polish general election.*
August	First non-communist government formed in Poland since 1945. The new Prime Minister (Tadeusz Mazowiecki) was a member of Solidarity. Gorbachev sent his congratulations. (Lech Walesa was elected President of Poland in December 1990.)
September	*Thousands of East Germans crossed to freedom in the West using the open border between Hungary and Austria.*
October	Demonstrations took place in both East Germany and Bulgaria. Gorbachev told the East German leader to reform. A non-communist government was established in Hungary.
9 November	*Berlin Wall was taken down.*
10 November	Bulgarian President resigned.
24 November	*Communist government of Czechoslovakia was overthrown following protests and a general strike which brought the country to a standstill.*
December	East German government resigned. A new non-communist government was formed in Czechoslovakia. Reforms agreed in Bulgaria eg. free elections. In Romania fighting led to the capture and execution of President Ceausescu and his wife. It was the only country to have a violent revolution against Communism.

The Berlin Wall comes down, 1989.

foundation in **Gdansk** of a free trade union called **Solidarity** which became a national force for change under its leader, **Lech Walesa**. One third of the Polish people, including members of the Communist Party, joined Solidarity, which was supported by intellectuals and by the Church.

Its aims were popular (eg lower food prices and the right to strike) but when, in December 1981, it demanded a referendum on the issue of the one-party system, the Soviets became worried. They did not send in troops but put pressure on the Polish government to take tough action. The leaders of the union were arrested and Solidarity was banned. However, it continued to exist underground and when **strikes** broke out in **January 1988**, Solidarity leaders met the government to negotiate. In 1989 Solidarity became legal and workers were granted the right to strike. Free elections followed and, by August, Poland had its first non-communist government since 1945.

The collapse of communist rule in Hungary, East Germany, Bulgaria, Czechoslovakia and Romania followed in rapid succession (see table opposite). Ironically, Eisenhower's 'domino theory' concerning the spread of communism, proved a more accurate description of its collapse in Eastern Europe (source F). The most dramatic event of these months, for people in the West, was the taking down of the Berlin Wall — that symbol of the iron curtain and lasting reminder of the division of Germany, and its importance in the Cold War (source E). While its empire in Eastern Europe collapsed, the Soviet Union did not intervene (source G). Gorbachev remained true to his promise of December 1988, and in **December 1989** he met President Bush in Malta where they made an historic announcement — **the Cold War was over**.

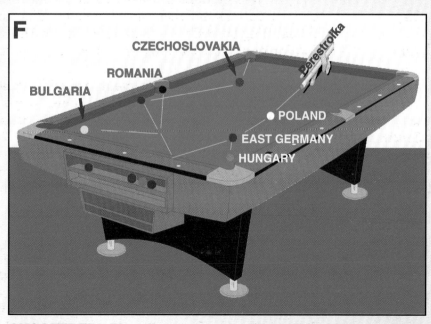

SNOOKERED! The collapse of communism in Eastern Europe. A variation on the domino theory.

59

?

1 With the help of source B, explain what Gorbachev hoped to achieve through his reforms.

2 Read sources A and H.
   (a) What did the Soviet people think of their leaders?
   (b) According to source H, how successful were Gorbachev's reforms?

3 Why did Gorbachev's reforms affect superpower relations?

4 Read source C. How did this speech mark a turning point in Soviet relations with the West?

5 In a web diagram, summarise the results of Gorbachev's policies.

G

A NEW DOCTRINE IS IN ITS PLACE WHICH IS THE 'FRANK SINATRA' DOCTRINE. FRANK SINATRA HAD A POPULAR SONG, I DID IT MY WAY. SO HUNGARY, POLAND AND ANY OTHER COUNTRIES HAVE IT THEIR WAY. THEY DECIDE WHICH ROAD TO TAKE. IT'S THEIR BUSINESS.

Gennady Gerasimov, of the Soviet Foreign Ministry, Autumn 1989.

SOURCE

H

1 THERE ARE THREE KINDS OF PERSON IN THE SOVIET UNION:
* *THE OPTIMISTS — THEY BELIEVE IN WHAT GORBACHEV SAYS;*
* *THE PESSIMISTS — THEY ARE LEARNING ENGLISH AND PLANNING TO EMIGRATE;*
* *THE REALISTS — THEY ARE TAKING RIFLE LESSONS AND GETTING READY FOR CIVIL WAR.*

2 THERE ARE TWO WAYS OF RESOLVING THE CRISIS IN THE SOVIET ECONOMY:
* *THE REALISTIC WAY — ALIENS FROM OUTER SPACE WILL LAND AND STRAIGHTEN OUT THE MESS.*
* *THE FANTASTIC WAY — THE SOVIET PEOPLE WILL SORT IT OUT FOR THEMSELVES.*

Two jokes circulating in the USSR in 1989.

SOURCE

The end of a superpower

At home Gorbachev faced growing problems. By 1990 the USSR was sliding into economic chaos. Decentralisation of industry did not work because local managers wanted to manufacture those products which yielded high profits. As a result, basic commodities such as soap, became scarce. Food distribution remained inefficient. Though the 1990 grain harvest was good, 40% was either left to rot in the fields or was eaten by rats. Thanks to broken down oil wells, the world's largest oil producer was about to become an importer. Rising inflation added to the difficulties and discontent. Glastnost did not restore confidence. It simply encouraged debate and criticism of the government (source H). Gorbachev's successes abroad failed to compensate for the problems at home.

In **July 1990** Gorbachev agreed to **German unification** within NATO. The reunification of Germany in October meant the end of the division of Europe. In **August 1991 START I** was finally signed by Bush and Gorbachev. Their countries agreed to destroy a third of their nuclear weapons. Unfortunately, by then nationalism within the Soviet Union had become an important issue. Gorbachev opposed the break up of the Soviet Union but **Latvia** and **Lithuania** had already declared themselves independent. As Moscow's control weakened, Gorbachev faced criticism both from those who thought he had made too many changes, and from those who felt he had made too few. An attempted coup against Gorbachev in August 1991 failed thanks to the support of **Boris Yeltsin** but, within months, the former Soviet Republics had decided upon independence. In **December 1991 Gorbachev resigned** as Soviet President and the **USSR ceased to exist**.

2.7 Conclusion — Cold War or Long Peace?

A

VIEWS ON THE END OF THE COLD WAR

GORBACHEV REALISED THAT THE SOVIET UNION COULD NO LONGER SUPPORT A FIRST-RATE MILITARY ESTABLISHMENT ON THE BASIS OF A THIRD-RATE ECONOMY.
Kenneth N Waltz, political scientist, 1993

THERE ARE FEW LESSONS SO CLEAR IN HISTORY THAN THIS: ONLY THE COMBINATION OF CONVENTIONAL AND NUCLEAR FORCES HAVE ENSURED THIS LONG PEACE IN EUROPE.
President George Bush, 1990

WE'RE WITNESSING THE REWARDS OF THE REAGAN POLICY OF FIRMNESS.
Presidential adviser, Richard Perle, 1991

THE COLD WAR ENDED BECAUSE IT WAS NO LONGER FEASIBLE [POSSIBLE]. THE UNITED STATES AND THE USSR HAD EXHAUSTED THEIR CAPACITY TO CARRY ON THEIR GLOBAL CONFRONTATION . . .
Peter Gladkov, policy analyst, 1994

IT SEEMS LIKELY THAT INTERNAL PRESSURES PLAYED AS MUCH, IF NOT MORE, OF A ROLE IN CONVINCING THE SOVIET LEADER TO AGREE TO MEASURES THAT CUT HIS COUNTRY'S FIREPOWER . .
Carl P Leubsdorf, political journalist, 1991

SOURCE

B

THE PROBLEM IN DEFENCE SPENDING IS TO FIGURE HOW FAR YOU SHOULD GO WITHOUT DESTROYING FROM WITHIN WHAT YOU ARE TRYING TO DEFEND FROM WITHOUT

President Eisenhower, 1956

SOURCE

C

ABOLISHING NUCLEAR WEAPONS FOREVER WAS SIMPLY NOT POSSIBLE BECAUSE THE UNDERSTANDING OF HOW TO MAKE THEM WOULD ALWAYS REMAIN.

Mandelbaum and Talbott,
Reagan and Gorbachev, *1987*

SOURCE

The collapse of communism in Eastern Europe was seen by some in the West as a victory for America and for capitalism. It was argued that Reagan's tough tactics in the early 1980s had paid off. The Soviet Union had been unable to keep up with its rival in the arms race and so was defeated (source A). However, the pressures of the arms race were not the sole reason for the break-up of the USSR. Its relatively sudden collapse was due to a breakdown of central authority in Moscow, and that in turn was brought about by Gorbachev's reform programme. Sweeping change brought economic chaos, criticism and instability.

The cost of rivalry
The Soviet Union clearly paid a very high price for its defence and foreign adventures during the Cold War. The speed of its collapse high-lighted the USSR's basic weakness, which its military power had effectively hidden since 1945. The Americans could afford to fight the Cold War on the one hand, while making money with the other. In 1945 they had the advantage of the richest economy in the world, while the Soviets faced the daunting task of rebuilding their country, which had been devastated by war. Thanks to the persistent problem of low productivity, combined with high defence budgets, the USSR never did catch up. It remained 'an incomplete superpower'.

The Cold War began in Eastern Europe and ended there. Once the USSR agreed to allow its East European satellites to choose their own form of government, communist rule collapsed and Europe ceased to be divided by an iron curtain. The issues which had so quickly driven the wartime allies apart in 1945 were no longer relevant. Free elections were now allowed; the Soviet army of occupation withdrew; Germany was reunited and fears of the spread of communism receded. With the collapse of the USSR itself in 1991, there was only one super-power left. The longstanding rivalry between America and the Soviet Union, which had dominated international relations since 1945, had come to a surprisingly quick end.

Yet America also paid heavily for its commitment to the Truman Doctrine and the policy of containment. Its casualties in Korea and Vietnam; the loss of confidence after defeat by the Vietcong; the sense of guilt over the horrific treatment of Vietnamese villagers, both young and old, were all part of that price. Moreover, even the American economy could not sustain huge defence budgets indefinitely. In 1980 the USA was the world's largest creditor and its national debt was one trillion dollars. By 1992 it was the world's largest debtor, with a national debt of four trillion dollars. Reagan's increased

An American cartoon from 1992.

defence budgets and SDI were mainly responsible for such a dramatic change of fortune. Eisenhower had recognised the problem in the 1950s (source B).

While the two superpowers bore the crushing burden of the arms race and provided protection for their allies and satellites, countries like Japan were free to invest both in industry and in research into consumer products. When the Cold War ended, Japan was the richest country in the world with the highest per capita income, hence the comment from one of the candidates in the 1992 US Presidential election: "The Cold War is over — and Japan won." The end of the Cold War freed both superpowers from a rivalry which was a huge drain upon their economies.

The development of nuclear weapons also had an unforeseen and dangerous effect upon the environment. Damage from weapons testing (eg in the Pacific) raised concern, while accidents at nuclear plants, such as Three Mile Island, Pennsylvania (1979) and Chernobyl, Ukraine (1986) attracted world wide attention and highlighted the dangers of reliance upon nuclear power. The nuclear fall-out from the Chernobyl explosion equalled that of ten Hiroshima bombs and poisoned an area the size of Holland.

Cold war or long peace?

The importance of nuclear weapons in the Cold War meant that the post 1945 generation grew up under the threat of a nuclear holocaust. Pictures of the devastation of Hiroshima and Nagasaki in 1945 provided vivid images of what to expect in a nuclear war between the superpowers. The knowledge that the weapons of the 1980s were infinitely more powerful and deadly than the original atom bombs fuelled fears and increased support for the campaigns for nuclear disarmament. However that aim itself was unrealistic (source C).

In fact the superpowers were increasingly aware of how each had the potential to destroy itself as well as its opponent in a nuclear war. Though the USSR's nuclear arsenal did not match that of the USA until the 1970s, it still had sufficient weapons to destroy America. Realisation of their mutual danger acted as a restraint upon both superpowers. Despite their hostility they carefully avoided military confrontation and its consequences. They developed their own rules of conduct (eg each respected the other's sphere of influence). Though both threatened the use of nuclear weapons during the 1950s, the Cuban crisis frightened them enough to abandon such tactics.

Therefore the 40 years of Cold War could be regarded as years of peace and stability, especially when compared to the two world wars fought earlier in the century. The wars in Korea, Vietnam and Afghanistan were fought in a limited area, using conventional weapons and only one superpower was directly involved at any time. As long as America and the USSR were perceived as giant superpowers by the rest of the world they could dominate international affairs, dictate policies and manage crises entirely in their own interests. Above all they could preserve the uneasy peace which lay between them. The combination of danger and crippling expenditure upon defence prepared both sides for détente.

The end of the Cold War brought freedom to Eastern Europe, the abolition of the Warsaw Pact and the abandonment of SDI. It also allowed the UN to make its first united response to aggression in 1991, because the USSR and USA agreed with the decision to use force to drive the Iraqis out of Kuwait. Throughout the UN's history the rivalry between the superpowers had prevented such co-operation. Economic issues now became the priority as is usual in peacetime. However, the end of superpower rivalry did not divert more money to the Third World or stop regional wars.

The revival of nationalism in the communist bloc not only led to the break up of the USSR, but also to the division of former Czechoslovakia and Yugoslavia, where a vicious civil war was fought (source E).

The nuclear threat remained but now the weapons of the Soviet Union were dispersed among the former Soviet republics. The new republics of Ukraine and Belarus refused to ratify **START I**. Though **START II** was **signed** in **January 1993**, it could not come into effect until **START I** was ratified. Third World countries, which had previously relied upon a superpower for defence, increased their production and purchase of arms, while

humanitarian causes such as medical care were neglected. The failure of the **Non-Proliferation Treaty of 1968** meant that as more countries acquired nuclear weapons, the danger of nuclear war grew. Fear of communism had united the West but, without the USSR as the common enemy, the allies fell apart. In the former Eastern bloc countries, people became disillusioned with the so-called benefits of democracy and capitalism and voted the communists back into power.

The end of the Cold War may have been hailed as a triumph for capitalism, but it also brought instability to threaten world peace once more. At Fulton, Missouri, where Churchill delivered his famous 'iron curtain' speech in 1946, Gorbachev acknowledged that both sides made mistakes in the early post-war years but added
"It would be a supreme tragedy if the world, having overcome the 1946 model, were to find itself once again in a 1914 model."
(Mikhail Gorbachev, 6 May 1992.)

F

FORMER SOVIET UNION STATES

1985

Brazil, Iran, Pakistan, South Korea
Argentina, BELGIUM, ITALY, Taiwan
Israel, JAPAN, South Africa, West Germany

1975

INDIA

1965

CHINA

FRANCE

1955

USSR   UK

USA

1945

USA	Major nuclear powers
INDIA	Capable of producing 30+ weapons
Argentina	Capable of producing a few weapons

Countries which have, or are believed to have, the capability of making nuclear weapons 1945-91.

?

1 "The years of the Cold War between the superpowers brought no benefits." Do you agree? Explain your answer.

2 What do sources D, E and F suggest about the world after the Cold War ended?

GLOSSARY

ABM: anti-ballistic missile which could intercept and shoot down enemy missiles.

Allies: countries which agree to help and defend each other.

Atomic bomb: the first nuclear bomb.

Balance of power: Where two countries or groups of countries have equal power.

Bloc: a group of countries with the same aim or interest.

Blockade: where a place is surrounded so that nothing and no-one can get in or out.

Capitalism: a system where property is owned by individuals, not the state, and they can become rich.

CIA: Central Intelligence Agency of spies for the USA.

Cold War: the years 1945 to 1990 when the two superpowers hated each other but stopped short of fighting.

Comecon: Council for Mutual Economic Aid was the USSR's answer to the Marshall Plan in Eastern Europe.

Cominform: Communist Information Bureau aimed to increase support for the USSR within Eastern Europe.

Communism: where the state is controlled by the communist party and there is no private property.

Congress: the US parliament.

Containment: US policy whose aim was the stop the spread of communism.

Coup: a seizure of power.

Covert: secret.

Crisis: a dangerous situation.

Democracy: where a country's leaders are elected by the people.

Détente: an easing of tension between the superpowers.

Dissidents: people who disagree with their system of government.

Doctrine: public statement of policy.

Domino theory: how communism would spread, causing governments to fall like dominoes.

Economy: the way a country earns or creates wealth.

Free elections: where people vote in secret for the party of their choice.

Fundamentalists: people who hold strong, traditional religious beliefs.

Glasnost: openness to different views, freedom of speech and an end of censorship.

Guerrilla warfare: using tactics like ambush, hit and run etc, against a more powerful enemy.

H-bomb: hydrogen bomb which was a thousand times more powerful than the atomic bomb.

ICBM: inter-continental ballistic missile which had a range of 1500 – 8000 miles.

Ideology: a set of political beliefs.

Inflation: rising prices.

Iron curtain: term used to describe the border between the Soviet bloc and the West.

KGB: Soviet spies.

Marshall Aid: US plan to help European economic recovery.

MAD: Mutual Assured Destruction of both superpowers in a nuclear war.

MIRV: multiple independently targeted re-entry vehicle was a missile with many warheads which could be fired at widely separated targets.

NATO: North Atlantic Treaty Organisation formed to resist communism.

Neutral: not supporting either side.

Nuclear deterrent: possession of nuclear weapons would stop the enemy using its nuclear missiles.

Perestroika: reorganisation of the Soviet state and economy for the benefit of the people.

Prague Spring: brief period of reform in Czechoslovakia in 1968.

Ratify: approve.

Reparations: compensation.

Satellite: a country controlled by a superpower.

SEATO: South East Asia Treaty Organisation formed to resist communism in that area.

Second strike capability: the ability to return fire in a nuclear attack.

Security: defence of a country.

Sphere of influence: general area controlled by a superpower.

Sputnik: space satellite.

SALT: Strategic Arms Limitation Treaty.

SDI: Strategic Defence Initiative nicknamed 'Star Wars'.

START: Strategic Arms Reduction Treaty.

Summit: Meeting of world leaders.

Treaty: an agreement signed by two or more countries.

UN: United Nations Organisation aimed to maintain world peace.

Vietcong: Vietnamese nationalist (and communist) army which fought the Americans.

Vietnamisation: Nixon's policy of gradual withdrawal of US troops, giving control of the war to the South Vietnamese.

Warsaw Pact: defence alliance of East European countries.

Zone of Occupation: area of Austria, Germany and Berlin occupied by the army of one of the four allies.